THE ASTROLOGY OF RELATIONSHIP

The Astrology of Relationship

A HUMANISTIC APPROACH TO THE PRACTICE OF SYNASTRY

by Michael R. Meyer

ANCHOR BOOKS

ANCHOR PRESS/DOUBLEDAY, GARDEN CITY, NEW YORK
1976

The Anchor Books edition is the first publication of
THE ASTROLOGY OF RELATIONSHIP.
Anchor Books edition: 1976
Illustrations by Michael R. Meyer
Calligraphy by Nancy Kleban
Portraits on pages 191, 211 and 231
by Armando Busick

Library of Congress Cataloging in Publication Data

Meyer, Michael R.
    The astrology of relationship.

Bibliography: p. 259
    1. Astrology.   I. Title.
BF1708.1.M474   133.5
    ISBN 0-385-11556-3
Library of Congress Catalog Card Number 75-44528

To NANCY

a companion on the path of transformations

CONTENTS

Part One

THE MYSTERY OF HUMAN RELATEDNESS

1   *The Evolution of Astrological Consciousness*   13
2   *The Nature of Relationship*   31

Part Two

THE ASTROLOGICAL SYMBOLS
OF RELATIONSHIP

3   *Synastry and the Symbolism of Relationship*   53
4   *The Planets*   65
5   *Planetary Phases and Aspects*   81
6   *The Houses*   109
7   *The Signs*   127
8   *Planetary Combinations*   145

Part Three

SYNASTRY: A GUIDE TO
UNDERSTANDING RELATIONSHIP

9   *The Techniques of Synastry*   169
10   *The Practice of Synastry*   189

Bibliography   259

FOREWORD

I would like to extend my thanks to all those who helped in the production of this volume. I'm particularly indebted to Nancy Kleban whose sensitive editorial and graphic assistance contributes much to its coherency and aesthetics. I would also like to express my gratitude here to Armando Busick, Gery Giannandrea, Robert Grantham, Estrella Milner, Tony Milner, Dane Rudhyar, and Stuart Zinner for their helpful comments and encouragement.

Part One

THE MYSTERY OF
HUMAN RELATEDNESS

1. THE EVOLUTION OF ASTROLOGICAL CONSCIOUSNESS

Scientists, philosophers, and artists have contemplated for centuries the interactions between macrocosm (greater whole) and microcosm (lesser whole) that bring into manifestation both the visible and the invisible realms of the universe. A fundamental principle of nature, recognized by sages of all times, is that all things—from galaxies to human beings to atoms—interrelate and interpenetrate. "Everything exists for itself," according to physicist-psychologist Wilhelm Reich, "yet everything is a part of something else." The ancient system of knowledge known as astrology is essentially an application of this awareness: because human beings (and all forms of life on Earth) and the solar system are parts of the same whole, there must be a correspondence of some kind between the cyclic motions of the celestial bodies and life on this planet.

In early phases of mankind's development, "astrology," if we can call it that, operated as instinctual rather than as rational, conscious knowledge. People were naturally more active during the day than at night, long before they were able to use a thought process to come to the conclusion that the sun was visible in the sky radiating light and heat during the day and that their world was dark and cold with the sun's absence during the night. Modern researchers have been studying similar patterns in the animal and plant kingdoms. They are finding, generally, that many animals and plants are attuned with the cyclic motions of the sun, moon, and planets.[1] Even such a simple creature as the ant apparently has the ability to calculate its relative geographical position on the surface of the Earth from its perception of the sunlight—with the speed and accuracy of a computer!

As human beings began to develop keener mental abilities and evolved a sense of individuality, they gradually lost their sense of unity with the universe. In the process of becoming an individual, self-conscious entity capable of using and developing mental powers, man (in the generic, collective sense of the word) lost the instinctual ability to flow with the rhythm of nature. This placed humanity in an awkward and potentially dangerous position. Human beings became unique members of the universe when they were able to consciously separate themselves from it and analyze it. It was probably then that the intellectual, analytical type of astrology began to emerge as a tool to assist humanity in coping with the environment.

No one really knows when and where the traditional ideas and concepts underlying astrology as we know them today were first practiced. Many astrologers believe that some early kings of Egypt were avataric personages and the originators of astrology, or at least high initiates into occult knowledge. The remarkable complexity of the Great Pyramid demonstrates that at the time of its construction (estimates range from 4,000 B.C. to 25,000 B.C.) there was in existence a type of astrological/mathematical knowledge very possibly exceeding that of our own day.[2] Similar achievements can be seen in Britain at Stonehenge and in some of the constructions of the Mayan civilization in Central America. It is widely believed among occultists that the ancient civilizations we know of today have unimaginably ancient roots—possibly going back to a great Atlantean civilization.

With the probable exception of its use in esoteric studies, astrology was essentially a guide used collectively for determining the most suitable time to plant and harvest crops, make war, collect taxes, and the like, until the sixth century B.C. About this time, in India and Greece, individual birth charts, drawn up for the time and place of a person's birth, became available to anyone who could pay the astrologer's fee. People were interested, as most are today, in obtaining astrologers' advice mostly about such things as financial matters, career opportunities, and romantic affairs.

The idea that astrology could be used in the realm of love and/or marriage particularly caught the fancy of astrologers and the public alike—and there developed a branch of astrology called "synastry" (*sny:* together, *astry:* star). Many cultures adopted the practice of synastry, and especially in India it was and still is held in the highest regard. In the Hindu culture love, marriage, and sex are regulated according to the advice of the family astrologer: An astrologer is on twenty-four hour call when a birth is due in order to assure an accurately timed birth chart. Often while children are still quite young, their spouses are selected on the basis of a comparison of horoscopes. The exact moment of the marriage ceremony, as well as the first sex act, is calculated to harmonize with the patterns of the celestial bodies.

ASTROLOGY TODAY

Astrologers still often play decisive roles in the realms of business, speculation, and particularly romance. The question concerning the practical use of astrology most frequently asked of astrologers is usually something like, "I'm an Aries and my boy friend is a Leo—does that mean we're compatible?" Astrologers are also often called upon to help a confused person decide which of a number of lovers would make the best match, or to help discover how a person might get what he or she wants from a relationship.

These questions and the use of astrology as a means of responding to such situations may seem valid to the reader. However, he or she should be aware that what is today almost universally recognized as all there is to astrology by the general public, and even by many astrologers, is actually a decadent form of astrology with an exaggerated concern for events and oversimplified methods.

For centuries, perhaps millennia, the only publicly known astrology was that which dealt with the prediction of events and the analysis of character. Any astrology that was concerned with individual growth, actualization, and transformation was strictly secret, as was the situation with alchemy; exoterically supposed to be the practice of transmuting baser elements into gold and silver, the real (or inner) goal of the alchemist was that of refining and transmuting his or her own nature from the base to the pure. There was a great difference, however, between the astrology and the alchemy of medieval times. Astrology had then already become quite decadent, and unlike the majority of alchemists, astrologers as a group (with Paracelsus and only a very few other exceptions) were almost totally caught up in the exoteric, mundane, and predictive side of the study.

Because astrology became so strongly identified with the prediction of events, both the Church and the academic community have condemned it during the past few hundred years, even though astrology was highly respected before the seventeenth century and has been supported by such great scientists as Francis Bacon, Johann Kepler, and Isaac Newton. The Church ruled that the doctrine of astrology was superstitious and contrary to free will, and the emerging scientific community called the theory that the planets are able to cause events on Earth "unscientific." As a result, astrology suffered a long period of disfavor in the Western world, particularly from some time in the seventeenth century until the latter part of the nineteenth century.

In 1875 H. P. Blavatsky announced her mission to promote an intelligent world-wide investigation of the spiritual phenomena prevalent in the mid-nineteenth century, as emissary for a trans-Himalayan lodge of adepts, and helped to form the Theosophical Society. She introduced to Europe and America at that time a profound psychological and spiritual reorientation—the entire impact of which we are just now beginning to understand, a hundred years later.[3]

In relation to Blavatsky's occult and oriental philosophies of karma, dharma, reincarnation, cyclic evolution, and her communication with adepts (those who have evolved far beyond humanity), astrology began to seem somewhat acceptable to the world at that time. Many artists, philosophers, scientists, and truth seekers gathered around Blavatsky and were inspired by her teachings. The re-establishment of astrology that took place during the last quarter of the nineteenth and the first part of the twentieth centuries was promoted largely by Theosophists, including Sepharial, Alan Leo,

Max Heindel, Charles Carter, Marc Edmund Jones, and Dane Rudhyar.

REORIENTATION

The first phase of the evolution of astrological consciousness to go beyond the previous predictive, materialistic uses of astrology began during the 1920s in America with the work of Marc Edmund Jones. His books present a careful re-examination of the concepts of astrology in the light of modern philosophy and psychology, particularly Alfred Adler's psychological theories. At first Jones was reluctant to make his work available to a wide public, disseminating his teachings almost exclusively through a series of classes and study courses organized as a modern version of the ancient mystery schools. Eventually, however, his works did reach the general public, and his books are now among the best available on astrological theory and practice.

The next phase in the process of formulating and making public an evolutionary astrology was initiated during the 1930s by the composer-poet-painter-occultist Dane Rudhyar, who synthesized Jones's new approach to astrology with the analytical psychology of C. G. Jung and fundamental occult teachings—particularly with what Rudhyar calls "the cyclic process," which has roots in Blavatsky's *The Secret Doctrine*.[4] Rudhyar did a great deal to bring Jones's pioneer work to public attention. In 1936 *The Astrology of Personality* was published, Rudhyar's integrated and thorough statement of an evolutionary, humanistic approach to astrology.

Because of the conservative tendencies of most astrologers, however, the new astrology advanced by Jones and Rudhyar did not really begin to catch on until the late 1960s, when many open-minded individuals seeking meaningful alternatives to conventional life styles and traditional knowledge began turning to astrology in their search for a more profound understanding of life.

A humanistic approach to astrology differs from the conventional in many ways. Rather than being concerned with the prediction of events, the humanistically oriented astrologer is interested in bringing out the underlying meaning of events and in discovering how it can be used to further the development of a person's potential, symbolized by his or her birth chart. This astrology recognizes no bad (or good) signs or planets, but considers all astrological factors as having a purposeful place and function in the general scheme of things. The birth chart is seen not as a collection of unrelated parts that the individual has to struggle to overcome, but as a whole pattern, or gestalt, of potentialities that may be actualized and integrated into the fabric of his or her personality.

A HUMANISTIC APPROACH TO SYNASTRY

The traditional approach to synastry has suggested the use of astrological techniques as a means of assisting individuals in the subtle exploitation and manipulation of their partners, friends, and lovers —in getting the most out of relationships for one's self. However, synastric techniques can be more valuable when applied humanistically in helping a person understand and actualize the constructive, transformative potentialities of relationship in a manner fulfilling to *both* partners.

In the humanistic approach, the astrologer is not expected to make judgments. He or she assists self-determination rather than taking charge of the individual's decision-making process. If one approaches synastry this way, simply comparing the birth charts of two individuals will not reveal whether a relationship will be a success or a failure, but one may be able to point out possible areas where either ease or difficulty might develop. A birth chart symbolizes individual potentialities. By comparing two birth charts (which should be done only after the charts have been studied individually) one can come to an understanding of the basic potentialities in a relationship and discover how they can be best fulfilled.

Essentially, humanistic synastric techniques can serve as guides to understanding how two or more persons can best function together, assisting one another's growth and transformation as individuals and participants in humanity's evolution.

KARMA, REBIRTH AND RELATIONSHIP

The birth chart is a map of the solar system at the exact time and place of a person's first moment of individual existence. One's unfoldment from that moment on is reflected in the motions of the macrocosm and is naturally connected to the past and to the future, immediate as well as distant, evolution of that macrocosm. Relationships can be approached here as vehicles of change and growth. In order to understand relationships in terms of the ongoing process that is the universe, however, we must first consider the principles of karma and reincarnation.

According to occult philosophy, everything that exists has life and is a part of a great scheme of evolution. This scheme includes everything, from sub-atomic particles to galaxies, but we'll limit our discussion here to what is most immediately relevant to the evolution of individual and collective human consciousness. An individual's consciousness has evolved through association, or identification, with a series of human vehicles or "incarnations" in the past and, before entering human evolution (in distant epochs), evolved through the animal, plant, and mineral kingdoms, as well as through forms of life about which modern science is yet unaware.[5] Our consciousness is continually evolving toward higher states and will eventually unfold far beyond the state most of us are in today.

When H. P. Blavatsky first began disseminating ancient knowledge in 1875, Westerners knew almost nothing about such things as spiritual evolution, karma, and reincarnation and were not aware of states of matter and consciousness beyond the physical. Even those few who understood some fragment of occult knowledge were often too much a part of the prevailing materialistic attitude of the time to have an integrated vision of occultism. Blavatsky spent several years in Tibet under the instruction of two remarkable members of the trans-Himalayan occult brotherhood, known as Morya and Koot Hoomi. Morya and Koot Hoomi are adepts, often referred to as "Masters" or "Mahatmas," people who through a long series of incarnations have evolved to a state of human perfection, still remaining in touch with a few persons in order to fulfill their functions as guardians of humanity's evolution for this particular cycle of planetary evolution—a cycle of many thousands of years in duration, now just in its earliest phases.

Blavatsky was instructed by Morya and Koot Hoomi as their emissary to the modern, Western-dominated world to introduce, in the English language, a coherent body of ancient teachings that demonstrates the cyclic, evolutionary unfoldment of matter and spirit. The purpose of her mission was to help elevate humanity above the narrow materialistic world view that has been so overwhelming during the past few centuries. Her function, she once cryptically said, was "to change the mind of the twentieth century."

Blavatsky teaches (see especially *The Secret Doctrine*) that our solar system is composed of seven interpenetrating states of consciousness that function through seven interpenetrating spheres of matter. Figure 1 illustrates this scheme, with obvious limitations.

This oversimplified graphic representation depicts the seven levels of matter and consciousness—densest at the bottom, most subtle on top. With a stretch of the imagination, the horizontal arcs can be understood to represent the concentric circles one would see looking at a cross section of the interpenetrating spheres divided along their common equator.

The *physical* sphere is the realm of action and sensation; the *astral* the realm of emotion and feeling; the *manas* sphere the world of thought divided into *rupa* and *arupa*—with form and without form, rational and irrational, knowing and understanding, concrete and abstract. Most of us are only conscious of activity on these three spheres. Beyond them, the *buddhic* sphere is the realm of intuition and compassion, the universal mind, while the *atmic* sphere is the realm of universal spirit—that "can neither be located nor limited" —vitalizing the buddhic consciousness. The *monadic* sphere is the field said to be occupied by the "sparks of the ONE Divine Flame."

Each of the seven states of matter and consciousness can be subdivided into seven substates, and, conversely, this entire scheme of spheres is but one of seven great spheres in a larger cosmic scheme.

At the present state of human evolution most people can perceive only the solid, liquid, and gaseous states of physical matter even though we are immersed in, surrounded by, and actually composed

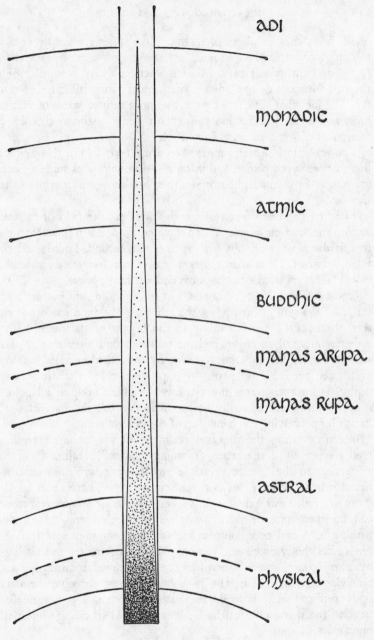

ADI

MONADIC

ATMIC

BUDDHIC

MANAS ARUPA

MANAS RUPA

ASTRAL

PHYSICAL

Figure 1

of, all forty-nine substates of matter. Most states are simply outside the range of our sensory organs, just as our eyes cannot perceive infrared and ultraviolet rays. Modern sciences today recognize only the three lowest, or most dense, of the forty-nine substates of matter. The fact that we cannot sense the more refined states of matter, however, is not justification enough for denying their existence, as many materialistic scientists have done.

The seven interpenetrating spheres are referred to in theosophical literature as seven planes, and in radical psychology as states of consciousness. In oriental philosophies they are known by various other names.

The first or most dense realm is the physical, the field of material action and consciousness. When divided into seven substates, the first is dense or solid physical matter; the second, liquid; and the third, gaseous. Finer than gaseous matter are four other substates called "etheric" by the theosophists and, by some, *prana*.

One's physical body is composed of solid, liquid, and gaseous matter from the skin inward while the etheric body (and its force centers, the *chakras*, corresponding to the organs of the dense body) radiates outward about an inch or more around all surfaces.[6] The etheric double can sometimes be seen by the naked eye and has now even been recorded on paper by a process called Kirlian photography. It interpenetrates and vitalizes the dense body at all points; it is the aura referred to by healers who can tell the state of one's health by perceiving the condition of the etheric body.

Interpenetrating the physical realm at all points and extending well beyond it is the astral (meaning "starry") realm, the *kama* (referring to the "desire principle" in Sanskrit writings) or emotional sphere. Science has not yet acquired the instruments to observe or record astral matter; it is so fine that a group of astral atoms can interpenetrate or pass through a physical atom without disturbing it. Astral consciousness includes our emotions and feelings; one's astral body or vehicle (composed of astral matter and vitalized by astral consciousness) serves as one's emotional transmitting and receiving center. Those who have been able to perceive the astral body report that it is ovoid and extends from one to several feet beyond the dense physical body. It is also said to change hue with one's emotional state.[7]

The *manas* sphere is the third state of matter-consciousness and is the vehicle of thought. It is differentiated into two functions: *rupa*, "having form," dealing with concrete thought and knowledge, and *arupa*, "without form," functioning on the level of abstraction, understanding, and archetypes.

It is difficult to conceive of any state of matter or consciousness more subtle than the mental. It is equally difficult to describe the nature of the buddhic, atmic, and monadic realms in words, expressions of concrete mentality. Concerning these, H. P. Blavatsky writes in *The Secret Doctrine:*

> [Buddhic], though a mere breath, in our conceptions, is still something material when compared with divine "Spirit" (Atma) of which it is the carrier or vehicle. Fohat [universal life energy], in his capacity of DIVINE LOVE (*Eros*), the electric Power of affinity and sympathy, is shown allegorically as trying to bring the pure Spirit, the Ray inseparable from the ONE absolute, into union with the Soul, the two constituting in Man the MONAD, and in Nature the first link between the ever unconditioned and the manifested. [p. 119]

The buddhic state of consciousness can be associated with compassion, the *intuitive* understanding of one's place and function in a planetary scheme of evolution and the ability to recognize and help fulfill the destiny of all other beings within this scheme. The atmic consciousness—the spirit that vitalizes buddhi—can be seen as a state in which spiritual *will* is capable of experiencing oneness with all. Monadic consciousness—the spark that is one with the "divine flame"—is associated with a consciousness that fully experiences all points of the universe simultaneously, while still retaining an individual focus. The finest realm is often referred to as *adi* ("the first impulse"), concerning which Blavatsky states, "naught can be said."

INDIVIDUALITY THROUGH THE CYCLE OF REBIRTH

A person is composed of several forms, or bodies, each vitalized by a particular type of consciousness. Because the various vehicles interpenetrate, they can also function independently. The three densest human vehicles are associated with acting (the dense physical and etheric), feeling (astral) and thinking (manas). These three bodies interpenetrate in much the same way as do solids, liquids, and gases on the physical plane. Just as liquids can be separated from solids, and gases can be separated from liquids, the feeling and thinking functions of human consciousness can operate independently of the physical body. The practice of astral projection is astral consciousness operating independently on the physical body. ESP is generally the ability to impress upon the physical brain the environment and experiences of the astral and mental spheres.

Personality, having been conditioned by culture, heredity, religion, etc., does not reincarnate. Though most people are totally identified with their personality or ego, it is not permanent or immortal. The physical body eventually dies and disintegrates, its remains returning to the elements. The astral body, or *kama rupa*, then also dies and disintegrates. The amount of physical time elapsing after the consciousness has completely separated from the physical body at death (a transition occurring on a temporary basis in sleep) until the death of the astral vehicle may be from a few minutes to decades or even centuries, depending upon how much vitality, desire, or inertia is retained by the astral body after physical death. The consciousness dwelling within the personality is then cut off from any physical experience, though still in touch with its own emotional life and that of those around it. A similar process takes place in the disintegration of the astral form, after which the personality is left with only its manas rupa vehicle. The duration of the personality's stay in the mental state, called *devachan*, may be from a few years to many centuries, depending largely on the evolution of its consciousness and needs on Earth's physical realm. Eventually, the entire personality including the lower mental vehicle disintegrates. At this time either a descent toward physical life commences or the conscious principle continues its "ascent."

Some questions naturally arise at this point: "What is it that reincarnates, what evolves into finer states, and how do these processes operate?"

Figure 2 represents the various principles or centers of human consciousness in terms of the seven spheres of nature. According to this scheme human consciousness is composed of three triads: per-

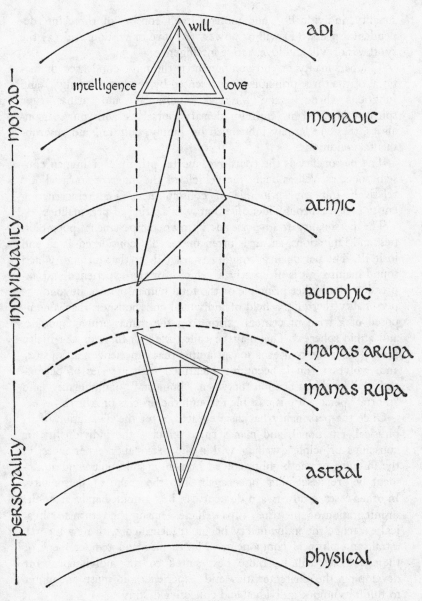

Figure 2

sonality, individuality, and monad. Each consists of three interdependent aspects: (1) will or power, (2) love or wisdom and (3) the synthesis of will and love, active intelligence.

The personality or ego component is the most condensed or material of the three principles (represented by the lower triangle) and functions through the physical, emotional, and manas rupa spheres. Most of us entirely identify ourselves with our personalities; they are largely influenced by family, cultural, and environmental conditions.

The personality is the transitive, mortal principle of human consciousness, as well as being the vehicle of the inner or spiritual and relatively immortal principle of consciousness. The reincarnating entity evolves through identification with a string of personalities.

The personality triad possesses its own temperament, potentialities, and limitations, and it is often mistakenly considered as an end in itself. The personality, roughly translated as "that through which sound manifests," is ultimately a vehicle for the experience and expression of a higher principle of the total human person. Beyond the personality there lies a field of individual consciousness that is composed of a triad of centers existing on the manas arupa, buddhic, and atmic spheres.[8] This may be called *individuality*, or the Ideity field. This is the reincarnating principle that experiences, assimilates, and evolves through becoming identified with a series of personalities. The identification between "immortal" individuality and "mortal" personality is possible through the process of rebirth.

Once the personality has disintegrated, after the dissolution of its physical, emotional, and manas rupa vehicles, the individuality or conscious principle dwelling within the personality experiences, in the instance of the highly evolved human, cosmic unity and atonement before descending once again into the realm of personality. In other cases, a downward descent can begin immediately after the disintegration of the manas rupa vehicle. During the return to physical existence the individuality becomes identified with new mental, astral, and physical components. The quality and temperament of these vehicles will be those best suited to the individuality for developing the characteristics and experiences it must encounter to fulfill its unique individual and collective destiny.

During the course of the lifetime of each personality, there occur many opportunities for unfoldment, presented in answer to the needs of the individual and/or the collective. How one responds to such needs, accepting and fulfilling them or rejecting them, greatly shapes subsequent experiences encountered by the personality as well as determines experiences the individuality will need to deal with through future incarnations. Within the context of this philosophy, this is the basis of karma. It is the implications of accepting or rejecting opportunity. Fulfilling a transformative opportunity leads one further along one's individual path of evolution, a path that is inevitably linked with a cosmic need. The rejection of an opportunity for transformation does not escape the need embodied; sooner or later a need for change must be dealt with. So-called "good" or positive karma is the result of harmonizing one's life and personality with the unfoldment of one's individuality and the needs of the cosmos. What is often referred to as "bad" or negative karma is, conversely, the results (often subjectively experienced as unpleasant) of one's efforts contrary to these needs. Karma operates on all levels of existence: personal, individual, national, collective, planetary, etc. The karma of an individual person is, furthermore, often subordinate to the karma of the nation, culture, etc., of which he or she is a part.

THE BIRTH CHART AS AN EXPRESSION OF KARMA/DHARMA

Karma is just one pole of an axis; its complement is *dharma*. Karma—the manifested order of things in the "here and now"—is connected with the past and the implications existing between the past and the present and/or future; dharma—the essence or truth of all things—focuses on the future, to the way things ought to be when their potential is actualized and the implications existing between the future and the present and/or past. Being polar opposites, karma and dharma are closely interrelated, yet each possesses specific functions. Karma is the portion of the evolutionary path behind the individual, dharma is the path leading the individual to the experiences necessary for evolution in harmony with his or her specific needs and the need of the cosmos for such an individual. Dharma is what one is born for.

The birth chart is a map of one's personal karma/dharma, a chart of the heavens at the completion of the rebirth process. The past (karma) of an individual calls forth the need to integrate certain experiences in the immediate future (dharma). In order to best fulfill these evolutionary needs the immortal individuality chooses and becomes identified with a personality in the making. The birth chart, cast for the birth moment of the physical body, is essentially a chart of the personality through which the individuality is operating. It represents the potentialities that should be developed during this particular incarnation. The chart of the personality, then, can be seen as a symbolic message to the individual, instructing it of the destiny it should fulfill through the personality.

Specific past or future incarnations or details of past or future experiences are not recorded in the symbolism of the chart, rather what has been integrated into the fabric of the individuality in the past, and what general types and qualities of experience should be fulfilled and integrated during the life span of the present incarnation, are indicated.

THE KARMIC IMPLICATIONS OF RELATIONSHIP

The study of relationship and the use of synastry to understand the deeper implications of human interaction take on new meaning in view of the workings of karma and rebirth when we realize that people often meet and participate together for the realization of a process that extends far beyond the lifetimes of their personalities. For instance, two individuals may become karmically linked through a series of incarnations in which their personalities form deep relationships that result in opportunities for contacts in future incarnations. There may be much to the romantic notion of "love at first sight" when we consider an intense reunion between lovers first brought together in new incarnations.

Just as karmic implications structure the web of destiny that brings people in contact with each other, underlying the immediate circumstances of a relationship there are dharmic potentialities ripe for actualization.

Every contact, no matter how incidental, between two persons (actually between one's self and everything one comes in contact with) is significant and serves the personality (and the individuality that stands behind it) by fulfilling a particular need in the evolutionary scheme. Some relationships, of course, are more karmically fertile and fruitful than others. Every relationship has its own quality and can be expected to bear its own special harvest. This does not imply, of course, that relationship, or a particular relationship, can ever be static. Each relationship has its own consistent nature, yet it is also constantly changing and transforming.

In natal astrology a person's archetypal pattern of *being* is represented by his or her birth chart while the individual process of *becoming* is symbolized by the progressed chart. The comparison of the birth and progressed charts of two or more persons can assist in reaching a deeper understanding of the quality, potentials, and focus of an interpersonal relationship, as well as guiding us to a closer attunement with the dynamic, transformative needs of our contacts. Synastry can help us understand the basic karmic implications of a relationship and can suggest how its dharma, or potential, may be actualized.

NOTES

1. Findings of researchers concerning the attunement of plants and animals to planetary cycles are presented in *The Secret Life of Plants* by Peter Tompkins and Christopher Bird (New York: Harper & Row, 1974); *Biological Clocks* by Frank Brown, J. Woodland Hastings, and John Palmer (New York: Academic Press, 1972); and *The Living Clocks* by Richie R. Ward (New York: Knopf, 1971).

2. Detailed reports of the astrological/mathematical wonders built into the Great Pyramid and Stonehenge can be found in Peter Tompkins' *Secrets of the Great Pyramid* (New York: Harper & Row, 1971); John Michell's *The View Over Atlantis* (New York: Ballantine, 1973); and *The City of Revelation* (New York: Ballantine, 1974).

3. A recent interpretation of Blavatsky's mission and teachings can be found in Dane Rudhyar's *Occult Preparations for a New Age* (Wheaton, Ill.: Theosophical Publishing House, 1975).

4. First published in 1888 (and currently available in several editions including a paperback abridgment), *The Secret Doctrine* introduced the concept of cyclic evolution to the Western world. For a detailed presentation of the cyclic process see also, Rudhyar's *The Planetarization of Consciousness* (New York: Harper & Row, 1972).

5. Detailed presentations of the seven states of matter and related points can be found in Blavatsky's *The Secret Doctine*, as well as in many of the works listed in the Bibliography in the Occult Philosophy section.

6. The chakras have been described as vortices or energy centers, part of the etheric body and closely related to the organs of the dense physical body. See C. W. Leadbetter's *The Chakras* (Madras, India: Theosophical Publishing House, 1927 and 1968).

7. A report on the nature and characteristics of the astral body prepared by two clairvoyants can be found in Annie Besant and C. W. Leadbetter's *Man, Visible and Invisible* (Madras, India: Theosophical Publishing House, 1902 and 1971).

8. There are several valid approaches to the representation of the principles of human constitution other than the one illustrated in Figure 2. In *The Secret Doctrine, The Key to Theosophy*, and elsewhere H. P. Blavatsky explains the septenary division of man according to the "trans-Himalayan" school. Such a scheme is composed of an upper, spiritual, immortal triad of atma, buddhi, and the dual (rupa and arupa) manas, and a lower, mortal quaternary made up of the kama rupa (astral body), prana (the vital principle that animates the etheric double and in turn the dense physical body), the linga-sarira (or etheric double), and the sthula-sarira (the dense physical body).

2. THE NATURE OF RELATIONSHIP

Of the many experiences and activities considered by astrologers, it is relationship that is the most encompassing and, today, the most in need of transformation. It is becoming clear that our conventional attitudes toward relationships among persons, nations, sexes, and that between humanity and the Earth as a whole, must be changed if we are to survive. The negative types of relationship that are so apparent today—war, imperialism, racism, sexism, and the gross exploitation of the Earth's material resources—may be bringing about one of the darkest eras in the chronicles of mankind. This situation is calling forth from human consciousness a deeper understanding of the function of relationship and a transformation of our traditional attitudes toward it—including our attitudes toward ourselves, the nuclear family, and the role we envision humanity fulfilling in terms of the Earth as a whole.

SELFHOOD AND RELATEDNESS

One of the two poles of existence is self. The factor of *selfhood* is the permanent element that structures the essential rhythm and power at the foundation of an existential whole, making it individual and distinct. The converse pole is the experience of being related to other selves. *Relatedness* is the factor of continuous change brought about through contact with others. The awareness of self and other is the most primary reality of human existence. Selfhood and relatedness were compared by Dane Rudhyar to the two foci of an ellipse—the pattern or curve of existence being determined by the interaction of these two factors, each a center of attraction exerting a basic pull. Although these two centers appear to be acting in opposite directions, both are essential to existence. Their pulls account for the cyclic structure of the process through which all forms of life evolve—on the vast cosmic level as well as that of subatomic particles.

Everything that exists, then, is both a thing in its *self* and an *other* from the perspective of all other selves. The interaction between self and other operates everywhere, on the horizontal as well as vertical levels. Like the Yin and Yang of ancient Chinese philosophy (see Figure 3), the two polar opposites are always in motion, always interacting, and are responsible for producing the manifest universe. The Tao—the universal principle of oneness and harmony—underlies their apparent duality.

Figure 3

THE TRANSFORMATIVE FUNCTION OF RELATIONSHIP

The constant interplay between self and other, between Yin and Yang, is not without meaning. Its purpose is to bring the universe and all that exists within it closer to a state of perfection. The experience of relationship brings about deep transformations in the psyche of a person. If something were born and lived in a vacuum, separated from and unrelated to everything, it would remain totally unchanged, in a state of inertia. Selfhood incorporates inertia along with potential; it is only through relationship that the potential aspect of selfhood can be actualized. Through relatedness a person can discover who he or she truly is and is not. The realm of relatedness is the way of transformation and evolution.

Discrimination is, of course, an important factor: The path of transformative relatedness naturally stresses quality and understanding in relationship rather than quantity. The realm of relationship has always been a source of great confusion, probably because of our inevitable tendency to analyze, manipulate, and exploit our relationships—processes that generate even greater confusion. A true understanding of relatedness lies outside the scope of strict dualism. If we wish to grasp the significance of relationship, or of a particular relationship existing between two fields of experience and activity, a holistic approach is called for, one that views relationship as a synthesis of life fields. A chemist interested in the nature of water studies the synthesis or combination of two atoms of hydrogen with one atom of oxygen (see Figure 4). Analyzing these atoms of hydrogen and oxygen separately will not reveal much about the nature of water, though it will tell the chemist something about the nature or selfhood of the elements involved. In order to study the nature of water, he must bring the elements together. When a synthesis of two elements takes place—be they atoms, human beings, or galaxies—a third factor emerges; something new is created that partakes of the nature of the two constituent elements, yet is something more. The exact nature of such a synthesis is unpredictable—except when the operation is rigidly repeated under identical and therefore artificial conditions.

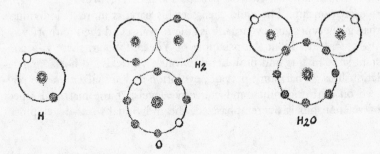

Figure 4

TWO TYPES OF RELATIONSHIP

There are essentially two types of relationships; *vertical* relationships that link individual fields in a hierarchical fashion, and *horizontal* relationships existing between individuals on the same level.

The interactions between the macrocosm and the microcosm are expressions of vertical relatedness. A person is an individual entity, a specific field of activity, at the same time he is a part of his family, community, culture, etc. His network of relationships with these larger wholes is structured in a vertical fashion: The individual person is also a part of a group of individuals. In *The Planetarization of Consciousness*, Rudhyar refers to this type of contact as a "matricial relationship." It begins physiologically in the prenatal state when the fetus is growing through the assimilation of the mother's substances. Matricial relationships continue to operate long after birth, developing on the levels of the mind, feelings, and psyche. A network of relationships evolves connecting a person's needs from his family, culture, and society, and their expectations of him.

While vertical or matricial relationships compose a network of contacts between macrocosms and microcosms, horizontal or associative contacts occur more consciously and deliberately on a person-to-person level, most intensely in the relationship existing between lovers.

At certain points, horizontal and vertical relationships intersect. To a child, for instance, parents are initially experienced more as archetypal figures of motherhood and fatherhood more than as individuals. But as he matures, the matricial, hierarchical relationship he has been having with his parents should transform to an associative relationship. The child then sees his parents more as individuals than archetypes and eventually is able to transcend their authority.

As we learn from the principle of Yin and Yang, there is a constant state of flux and flow between one's vertical and horizontal relationships. If harmony prevails, evolution and actualization are realized on both individual and collective levels. If the matricial aspect of relationship is overemphasized, the individual's self-development is in danger of becoming poisoned by an overdose of family or cultural substances. Conversely, when associative or horizontal contacts are too predominant, the family, culture, and society may be violated by an individual who has little regard for the well being of his community. Dane Rudhyar summarizes these principles in his work, *Directives for New Life:*

> The whole of society is based on relationship. The whole Earth is an immensely complex and integrated field of mutually interacting relationships. Human evolution is a series of changes in the basic character of interpersonal and intergroup relationships. [p. 71]

THE MALE-FEMALE POLARITY

The most essential differentiation between individuals acknowledged by humanity as a whole is that of sex. Every human being is biologically defined as being either male or female (including the few true hermaphrodites, although they possess more or less developed organs of both sexes). The strict division of the sexes in terms of physiology, psychology, and function, however, that is promoted by our Western culture is somewhat exaggerated. It is more likely that up until a few million years ago (a short span of time in relation to the vast cosmic cycles of evolution that occultists explore), there was not the division of the sexes that we know today.[1] Reproduction was achieved by means of a sort of fission. It was only at the most material and condensed state of human evolution (or perhaps *involution* is more precise here) that the distinct male/female division of humanity occurred. As humanity evolves further, according to some occultists, a synthesis or union of the sexes will once again be in order.

C. G. Jung commented on this artificial distinction in his book, *Two Essays on Analytical Psychology:*

> No man is so entirely masculine that he has nothing feminine in him. The fact is, rather, that very masculine men have—carefully guarded and hidden—a very soft emotional life, often

incorrectly described as "feminine." A man counts it a virtue to repress his feminine traits as much as possible, just as a woman, at least until recently, considered it unbecoming to be "mannish." The repression of the feminine traits and inclinations naturally causes these contrasexual demands to accumulate in the unconscious. No less naturally, the imago of woman (the soul-image) becomes a receptacle for these demands, which is why a man, in his love-choice, is strongly tempted to win the woman who best corresponds to his own unconscious femininity—a woman, in short, who can unhesitatingly receive the projection of his soul. [p. 189]

Deeply influenced by both ancient European and Asiatic occultism, particularly alchemy, Jung formulated the concept of anima/animus. His observations and the tradition of occultists are reflected in recent findings of biologists, demonstrating that every man has recessive female genes and female hormones circulating in his body as well as rudimentary female sex organs—and, of course, the converse is true of women—significantly expanding contemporary concepts of femininity and masculinity.[2]

ARCHETYPES OF THE FEMININE

Jung defines an archetype as an unconscious idea, image, or pattern of behavior that is universal—present in the psyches of all individual human beings. Among the innumerable archetypes of the collective unconscious are those that serve as symbols of human sexuality in general as well as the specifically feminine and masculine aspects of human sexuality.

In our Judeo-Christian culture women have occupied the lowest place on the totem pole of humanity. Images of virgin mothers, witches copulating with the devil, virgin brides of Christ, and the like introduced in this tradition are not real archetypes of the feminine, but complexes emerging from a repression of natural sex drives and a sense of fear-ridden guilt concerning most anything with sexual or sensual overtones. To discover truer archetypes of the feminine, we have to search outside of the Judeo-Christian tradition, to explore the *mythos* of ancient Egypt, India, China, and Greece. These cultures represented the feminine aspect, of nature as receptive, yielding, enclosing, form-giving, and reflective. It is a symbol for human feelings, emotions, instincts, and intuitions.

A fourfold typology of the feminine is presented by Toni Wolff in "Structural Forms in the Feminine Psyche."[3] The four types, summarized below (with some revisions), are operative in every woman's psyche (and in every man's anima). One or two of these archetypes is usually more predominant in one's psyche than the others, having what Jung would call a "superior function," while the others operate along more subtle and unconscious lines (see Figure 5).

Figure 5

The Mother symbolizes the functions of protection, nourishment, homemaking, and child rearing. In negative manifestations the Mother represents possessiveness, overprotectiveness, and interference. A woman predominantly of this type relates to a man through his social function as the family breadwinner rather than as an individual. She expects her children to adopt her social values and fulfill her demands/visions of how they should conduct their lives, rather than allowing them to experience life as self-determining individuals. She focuses her attention on a *person*, preparing him for a *collective* role. Demeter in Greek mythology and the Great Mother of Indian literature are symbolized here: nourishing and protecting or depersonalizing and devouring. In astrological symbology the moon represents the Mother.

The Daughter or *Sister* represents the sister, daughter, and lover aspect of the feminine—appearing in *mythos* as the love goddess: Hathor to the Egyptians, Aphrodite to the Greeks, and Venus to the Romans. She is opposite to the Mother in that she is oriented toward personal relationships and the unfoldment of herself and others as *individuals*. Ultimate love and personal interaction are the goals she strives to realize, avoiding confinement within a family or social structure. Her freedom to explore relationship and individual development is primary, superseding family and social responsibilities.

The Amazon archetype is oriented toward objective, cultural affairs and values, where individuality is fulfilled through a social (non-personal) responsibility, rather than through a mothering or interpersonal relationship. The Amazon woman relates to a man more as a partner or competitor than as a submissive wife or lover. In a negative manifestation she can be overefficient and insensitive to relationship and emotional needs. In Greek *mythos* she is seen as Athene and Artemus. In astrological symbolism she is represented by the planet Mercury.

The Medium or *Wise Woman* symbolizes the deeply subjective, intuitive, non-personal aspect of nature. She is open to the subtle and intangible elements of life. In negative manifestations she represents the loss of identity and discrimination, while in positive manifestations she symbolizes the function of objectifying and bringing into individual significance unconscious and unseen worlds. The Greek Pythoness is a possible representative of the Medium. She is symbolized in astrology by the planet Neptune.

ARCHETYPES OF THE MASCULINE

The masculine side of the human psyche complements and balances the feminine. It should be clear that both the feminine and masculine expressions of self are of equal value—though differing in function. They transcend distinctions of good/bad, strong/weak, and the like. The very existence of the feminine aspect demands the existence of a masculine to define it, and vice versa. Like the Yin and Yang of the Tai-Chi, feminine and masculine are simply two poles of the same axis.

The masculine aspect deals with action, thought, initiative, and self-exertion. While the feminine is ingoing and receptive, the masculine is outgoing, aggressive, and penetrating. All women, of course, have some masculine qualities included in their personalities. We are dealing here not with actual persons or even with the particular biological sexes, but with archetypal patterns of expression that are common, in varying degrees, to all humanity.

In his book on Jungian psychology, *The Symbolic Quest* (Harper & Row, 1969), Edward C. Whitmont applies a fourfold scheme to the masculine paralleling that of Toni Wolff. What follows is an outline of Whitmont's four expressions of the masculine with some adjustments of my own (see Figure 6).

The Father symbolizes structure and order, being the ideal leader, king, protector, and lawgiver—the upholder of social conventions and values. A man predominantly of this type sees women and children as wards or subjects more than individuals. In his negative manifestation the Father can be harsh and dogmatic. Moses and his anthropomorphic God are representatives of the Father archetype. In astrological symbolism he is represented by the planet Saturn.

The Son or *Brother* represents the companion, brother, son, and lover expression of masculine energy. In a sense he is the opposite of the Father as well as being the complement of the lover aspect of the feminine. He is more concerned with individual/personal expression and fulfillment than with social/collective demands. Dynamic, outward directed energy is at an apex here. Like the Daughter, the Son directs a good deal of this energy toward initiating relationships and seeking his own identity rather than in attempts at establishing his own social authority and permanence. In Greek *mythos* the Son is represented by some of the aspects of Dionysus, Ares, and Eros. The planet Mars represents him in astrological symbology.

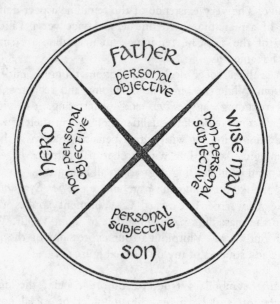

Figure 6

The Hero archetypifies the collective/non-personal aspect of the masculine. While the Son is oriented toward relationship and self-fulfillment, the Hero seeks outward achievements and social recognition. He is more concerned with establishing himself in a social or political context through great accomplishments than he is with discovering his personal identity and engaging in transformative interpersonal contacts. He typically sees women as partners in his success or obstacles in his path. Some expressions of Apollo and Hercules in Greek literature illustrate the Hero type. In astrology he is represented by the planet Jupiter.

The Wise Man or *Philosopher* typifies the individual who is more attracted to the realm of ideas and metaphysics than to those of family, passion, or ambition. He is a seeker of wisdom, a perceiver, a scholar, a teacher, and a sage rather than a ruler, lover, or administrator. The Wise Man is represented by the prophets of all traditions and by the planet Pluto.

ARCHETYPES OF UNION

The apparent duality of the masculine and feminine aspects of humanity is not irreconcilable. On the physical level masculine and feminine energies are synthesized in sexual union. Union need not be confined to the physical level, however; an integrated person can achieve an individual synthesis of this polarity personally, psychologically, and spiritually. The most familiar symbol of the union of masculine and feminine energies on the sexual as well as psycho-spiritual level is that of two interlaced triangles (see Figure 7). This symbol signifies the harmonious blending of two contrasting approaches to life and understanding.

Another archetype of the union of masculine and feminine expressions is provided by Hermaphroditus. Hermaphroditus was the son of Hermes and Aphrodite. His birth was concealed by his mother (he was an illegitimate god!), who entrusted the nymphs of Mount Ida with his rearing. Until he was fifteen years of age the youth enjoyed a half-wild forest life. One day the nymph Salmacis

Figure 7

saw Hermaphroditus bathing in a lake she ruled and was immediately enamored with his grace and beauty. She asked him to be her lover; he turned her down. Putting verbal formalities aside, the nymph then embraced him and lavished him with kisses, only to be resisted again. Salmacis, disappointed, begged all the gods to assure that nothing from that moment on would ever separate her from him. Their two bodies were united as one and in this form they were both man and woman. Whence the term hermaphrodite—describing those extremely rare instances in which a person possesses both male and female sex organs.

As an archetype the hermaphrodite plays an important role in the alchemical process called "the chemical marriage." As we noted, the alchemists of the Middle Ages operated under the front of transmuting base metals into gold and silver—an activity understandable and profitable to the materialistic mentality of their patron sovereigns. Their esoteric work, however, was to transmute their own base natures into states as pure as gold (symbolic of the sun and masculine energies) and silver (symbolic of the moon and feminine energies). This chemical marriage is a symbol of the perfect union of the feminine and masculine components of one's psyche and is often represented by the hermetic androgyne or the hermaphrodite. In an article titled "An Alchemical Allegory" published in *Maitreya 5*, Charles Poncé writes:

The hermaphrodite, in general, must be recognized as a symbolic expression of two different types of psychic orientation or consciousness . . . The figure of the hermaphrodite has been traditionally employed in the language of symbolism to demarcate the beginning and end of a process. [p. 20]

ASPECTS OF SEXUALITY

Of all the many organic functions of the human body it is sex that has most aroused curiosity, desires, fear, inspiration, and other innumerable human feelings. In spite of this fascination, we know really very little about sex. We know that sex differentiates male from female according to reproductive functions and that other more subtle distinctions are designated male and female, physiologically and psychologically. Sex also refers to the actual union between male and female—in the sex act, as well as in the urges, instincts, and intrigues associated with sexual union. Through the research of Alfred Kinsey, and more recently Masters, Johnson, and others, we have on hand a vast amount of statistical material concerning sex—the average frequency of intercourse, the average age of first sex act, the average number of orgasms one can expect to experience in a lifetime—the longest, the shortest, the most, and the least of anything connected with sex has been recorded by these and other diligent researchers. Handbooks describing various sexual techniques have become best sellers. Yet in spite of all our academic and technical information about sex, greatly needed and long over-due, we can communicate very little regarding the experiential and psycho-spiritual aspects of sex in its various manifestations. A person could read every one of the hundreds of volumes on sex, yet he or she might still be unable to comprehend the transformative experience of sexual love.

Much of the confusion and lopsided knowledge about sex may be rooted in an incomplete understanding of the various purposes of sex. In a prospectus for a book titled "What Is Sex For?" planned many years ago but never completed or published, Dane Rudhyar outlined three basic attitudes toward sex.

In the "biological-vitalistic" approach sex is an essentially non-personal, biological function, subservient to unconscious instincts and drives. Its sole purpose is reproduction. Sex operates in this form on all scales of existence.

In the "psychological-personal" approach to human sexuality, more prevalent in recent times due to the widespread availability of birth control, sex has nothing to do with reproduction or the urge to procreate. This use of sex is often conditioned by complexes and compulsions for personal gratification and the urge to release of psycho-mental tensions—often followed by the all too familiar possessiveness-jealousy syndrome. In its higher manifestations, sex can be a means of harmonizing and transforming the consciousness of the lovers.

The "sensate-aesthetical" approach to sex stresses the recreational aspect of sexual activity and has a capacity to fulfill "the very real need for refining man's and woman's capacity for keen sensation and nerve-response. It refers to sex as a glorified 'play.' "

In addition, I would suggest two more categories: The "electro-magnetic" approach, emphasizing sex as an exchange of vital human energies and magnetism. This type of sex stresses repolarization and healing. The "transpersonal-spiritual" approach stresses the union of lovers as a microcosm of cosmic reality and as a means of spiritual evolution. The true forms of tantric sex are of this type.

THE CIRCLE OF SEX

In his book *The Circle of Sex*, the late astrologer-sexologist Gavin Arthur developed a revolutionary scheme of sexual orientation. Since the book is out of print, I would like to present Arthur's concept at length here as a conclusion to this section on relatedness and sexuality.

The significance of Arthur's scheme lies in the fact that it is cyclic rather than linear. Alan Watts writes in the introduction that his work with the zodiac gave Gavin the notion

> that there may be 12 sexual types rather than two. Not just mommas and poppas, and outside these a disorderly mess of perverts and neurotics, but a rational spectrum of sexual varia-tions arranged in the form of a clock, which Gavin has called the Circle of Sex, and which was worked out with the sympa-thetic advice of such great sexologists as Havelock Ellis, Magnus Hirshfield and Alfred Kinsey. [p. 8]

Arthur's circle illustrates his principles, the twelve sections depict-ing twelve types of sexual orientation and temperament (see Figure 8). As is true of all natural cycles, the boundaries between one sec-tion and the next are blurred—each blends into the next. Just as in a rainbow, the colors of the spectrum gradually flow from one to the next, and in the circle of sex an infinite number of possibilities is represented. To personalize his twelve general sexual types, which should be regarded as archetypes found in varying degrees in everyone, Arthur has given them somewhat dubious names in an attempt to describe their nature. Arthur's circle of sex is simply one of many possible ways of presenting the various aspects of sexuality. My purpose in including the following outline of *The Circle of Sex* is to present the reader with a cyclic view of sexuality that in spite of its limitations may open new vistas to his or her understanding of this important facet of human psychology.

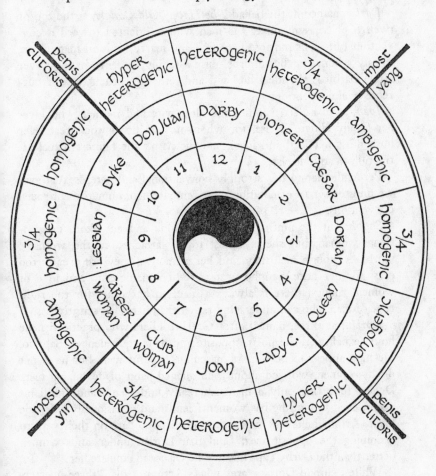

Figure 8

The central axis of the circle of sex is the vertical diameter, typifying the conventional, heterosexual, monogamous relationship between the male and female poles. Arthur explains that one could imagine the circle of sex "as the equator of a sphere. On this equator lie the 'hottest'—the most passionate—examples of each category. But toward the poles the categories merge into a common sexlessness, in which it is impossible to distinguish the categories clearly." [p. 32]

Darby, named in the ballad *The Happy Old Couple*, at the top or twelfth phase, symbolizes the man who is oriented toward a conventional life. His purpose is to find and marry his ideal mate, Joan, to buy a home in the suburbs, raise a family, and live happily ever after. Darby is the ideal husband and father according to our current social conventions.

Joan, at phase six, typifies the ideal wife and mother who loves her family above all else, for whom no sacrifice is too great. Her husband is her lord and ideal, and she hasn't the faintest sexual attraction to anyone else.

Perpendicular to this strongly conventional and heterosexual axis, we find the sexual orientation most removed from our present social conventions.

Sappho, in the ninth position, may look and act like a conventional woman, but she is almost totally attached to the woman's world. Although men may find her attractive, they are usually too crass for her taste. Sappho prefers the companionship and love of women, though there is always a place in her heart for the right type of man who can understand rather than harm her sensitivities.

Dorian, at three, named after Greek soldiers who practiced male homosexuality, is the polar opposite and male equivalent of Sappho. He may appear to be a most masculine type of man, but he is put off by women, worried about their alleged habit of devouring men. Dorian feels that only a man can really understand and fulfill his needs, even though he has women friends and occasionally a female lover. Arthur believes that Dorian and Sappho "are on their way to becoming the opposite sex," and that Dorian understands woman better than the Darby type because he wishes to emulate her.

While Sappho-Dorian are what Arthur calls "three-quarters

homogenic," if we follow the progression of the circle of sex in a clockwise direction, we come to the exclusively homogenic axis joining the tenth and fourth.

The Dyke, ten, is an obvious and exclusive female homosexual type and like her male equivalent, the Quean,* is most incongruous to our culture. Often dressing and acting as a man (although transvestites of either sex do not necessarily prefer homosexual relationships), the Dyke presents a masculine quality and is totally infatuated with the female sex. She is so devoted to women that she is repulsed by the thought of sex with a man, as much as a Darby is turned off by homosexual love.

The Quean, four, is the archetypal male homosexual who is not sexually attracted to women. Society makes life more difficult for him because of his unconventional life style than for those of any other sexual-psychological orientation. While the Quean's love relationships are exclusively with men, he often finds women interesting on the mental and philosophical level.

The cusp of the eleventh phase-fifth phase axis is a critical point in the circle of sex, comparable to the equinoctial axis of the zodiac. It is the physiological border between male and female.

Don Juan, phase eleven, has been described as the Dyke who has acquired a penis. He is the woman's man, so much attracted to women and their essence that he disdains most social contact with conventional men, or at least regards men in general as insensitive. The Don Juan type often appears effeminate and prefers the surroundings of the boudoir to those of the den. The polygamous life is his style, and he is more interested in giving his women orgasms than in sexual conquest as a means of demonstrating his masculinity.

Lady C., at phase five, named after Lady Chatterly and Catherine the Great, is the man's woman who enjoys hanging out with men and accompanying them on their adventures. Like the Don Juan type she may be mistaken for a homosexual. But also like the Don Juan, she is dedicated to heterosexual sex and often has something of a dislike for her own sex.

Continuing in a clockwise direction we come to the central axis depicted by Darby and Joan, who, as we saw earlier, represent the

* Quean is defined in the dictionary as "a woman of bad behavior."

pater-materfamilias—legitimate, monogamous, heterosexuality and the foundation of the traditional nuclear family.

The phase one-phase seven axis represents an orientation that is three-quarters heterogenic.

The Pioneer, at phase one, represents the type of man who enjoys working and functioning in the world outside of his home. Such a man has a large capacity for friendship with other men and enjoys the company of "the boys," though usually homosexual relationships are not usually what he's after. He tends to see women as essentially inferior to men, to a large extent as submissive sex objects and servants.

The Clubwoman, in the seventh section, is not primarily a homemaker. She enjoys outside social interests. This type of woman, possessing a mind of her own and cultural interests, if unable to find the type of companionship she needs from men, will seek friendship with other women.

The cusp of the phase two and phase eight sectors are points of maximal femininity and masculinity.

The Caesar, in phase two, is named after Julius Caesar, who was said to be every man's wife and every woman's husband. In spite of the fact that phase two is the most yang area in the circle of sex, the Caesar type is ambisexual. Although he usually comes on like a tough guy, he often represses his bisexuality and compensates by demonstrating his heterosexual prowess as a means of proving his outstanding masculinity. The Caesar type feels uncomfortable outside of his man's world—be it the factory, the ship, the battlefield, or the corner bar.

The Career Woman, eight, is typified by the feminine, glamorous woman who is attracted to men but forms deeper emotional attachments with women. This type is usually heterosexual and polygamous in practice.

The twelve sexual/psychological types represented in the circle of sex are archetypes of general sexual orientations. The area of human relationship and sexuality is a more complex field than is generally recognized: an infinite number of variations exists, changing from moment to moment. Once this is better understood perhaps we will be able to dispel the all-too-common belief that only conventional sexuality and relationships are "normal," while any deviation from the norm is perverted and illicit. Blanche M. Baker puts it aptly in her prologue to *The Circle of Sex:*

> It is regrettable that all too many people think of sex in terms of absolute dichotomy: men are male and women are female. Yet it takes very little observation to perceive that every person is a mixture of maleness and femaleness. . . . Nature does not deal strictly with black and white, for in between them spread all the colors of the rainbow. [p. 5]

NOTES

1. Rudolf Steiner's *Cosmic Memory* (current edition: Rudolf Steiner Publications, 1971) discusses occult teachings on the division of the sexes. See also *The Secret Doctrine*.

2. For a thorough study of the nature of physical sex, see *Sex Energy* by Robert S. de Ropp (New York: Dell, 1969).

3. Toni Wolff's paper was privately in Zurich, 1966. Source: Edward Whitmont's *The Symbolic Quest* (New York: Harper & Row, 1969).

Part Two

THE ASTROLOGICAL SYMBOLS
OF RELATIONSHIP

3. SYNASTRY AND THE SYMBOLISM OF RELATIONSHIP

The fundamental idea behind astrology is that the cyclic motions of the planets (the sun and moon included) correspond—though not necessarily in a causal fashion—to the life experiences of human beings and, on a larger scale, to all life within the Earth's biosphere. These motions are viewed from a geocentric (*geo:* earth, *centric:* centered) perspective, since human beings live on the Earth. The positions of the planets are plotted against the backgrounds of a variety of frames of reference.

ASTROLOGY IS MORE THAN "SUN SIGNS"

The most widely recognized astrological frame of reference, against which every celestial object can be viewed, is the *ecliptic of the zodiac*, or the zodiac of signs. The ecliptic is the *apparent* path of the sun around the Earth, a phenomenon actually produced by the Earth's yearly orbit around the sun. The ecliptic is a cycle of 360 degrees. It begins and ends at one of the two opposing points where the celestial equator (a projection of the terrestrial equator into space) intersects it—the vernal point (or 0° Aries) where the sun is situated on the first day of spring in the northern hemisphere.[1] The ecliptic is divided into twelve equal sections of thirty degrees each, beginning at the vernal point and producing the twelve *signs of the zodiac*.

Because the sun is the most obvious object in the sky and because every thirty days (one-twelfth of a year) it enters a new sign, the zodiacal sign occupied by the sun on the day of one's birth is the most accessible of the many factors that compose a birth chart. If a person knows the day of his or her birth, it is easy to find out the corresponding "sun sign"—without having to consult an astrologer or a costly reference table. Almost all astrological readings published in newspapers and magazines are based on sun sign astrology. The "horoscope" columns (horoscope is more correctly used to mean a complete birth chart composed of all the positions of the planets in terms of several frames of reference) featured in most daily newspapers, for instance, simply divide all of humanity into twelve general categories according to the twelve sun signs and attempt to give advice, character analysis, and predictions from this information alone. The same is essentially true of the many books currently available popularizing astrological techniques for compatibility and sexual analysis. They give very generalized and often sensational characterizations of individuals and relationships based exclusively on sun signs. "The Scorpio male," for instance, was described as "potent and sex mad" and "the Virgo female" as being "interested in incest" in one recent publication of this type. (As if there's never been a man born between October 22 and November 21 who had a moderate interest in sex or a woman born between August 21 and September 22 who wasn't preoccupied by intrigues with her relatives!)

The use of strictly sun sign astrology in any form is misrepresentative of the real purpose and practice of astrology. An individual human being is composed of a finely patterned complex of functions and potentialities that needs to be viewed from an integrated and holistic perspective if it is to be perceived in a true light. Attempting to understand a pattern of selfhood and relatedness from the sun sign approach is like being concerned only with the health of your heart, totally disregarding the other organs and systems of your body that work together and are intricately related in the health of your whole person.

WHAT IS SYNASTRY FOR?

Each of us is an individual with distinct potentials and experiences. Yet no man is an island, and we are constantly in contact with our environment as well as each having, as an individual, a unique role to play within a universal scheme of evolution. As we explained in the preceding chapter, there are two poles of existence: selfhood and relatedness. Each of us is an individual linked with and *related* to his culture, which is, in turn, a part of humanity, which is a part of the planetary organism, which is a part of our solar system, and so on. In a similar manner, the various atoms, molecules, cells, tissues, and organs that compose our physical bodies are related in a hierarchical fashion. The macrocosm-microcosm relationship can be seen everywhere on all levels of existence. At the same time, each of us is also drawn to relationships that are not hierarchical, such as relationships with friends, partners, colleagues, and lovers.

Natal astrology—the astrology of the individual—is meant to serve as a guide for assisting individual persons in achieving a clear understanding of who and what they are, understanding their birth potential and how it can be fulfilled, as well as their function in a larger frame of reference: the function that they are meant to fulfill in a social, collective, global, and even cosmic sense. No one, however, can actualize such purposes in a vacuum. Actualization and transformation can take place only through relationship. In a cosmo-philosophical treatise called *The Planetarization of Consciousness*, Dane Rudhyar observes:

Every change is the result of some kind of relationship being altered. Every transformation in the consciousness of a human being can be traced to some relationship which triggered the need and the desire for transformation. Within any cycle of existence, self is the permanent factor, the changeless rhythm and essential character of the field of existence; but it is through relationship that changes occur, over and above this fundamental rhythm. It is through the energy released by associative relationship that the human person is able to grow and to actualize the inherent potentiality of conscious fulfillment in selfhood. [p. 95]

The purpose of synastric techniques in astrology is to assist individuals in understanding the potential and quality of their relationships. It is to explore how two or more persons (or entities) can combine their forces in such a way that both are enabled to grow and better actualize their birth potentials, as well as to encourage them to participate (both as individuals and as a collectivity) in a broader, transpersonal function.

Synastry cannot tell us everything about a relationship, no more than natal astrology can tell us every life event and personal characteristic in detail about a person. No astrological technique, no matter how thorough, can accurately reveal the past, present, or future events of a person's life. Likewise, synastry cannot tell us who will make an ideal mate, what a relationship with someone will be like, where there is a probability of homosexual relationships, or who is a terrific lover! Astrology, at least from a humanistic perspective, deals with potentialities and suggests the processes and experiences through which the potential can become the actual.

Synastric techniques can reveal the potentialities of a relationship existing between two or more individuals and the kind of mutual experience that can promote both individual and collective unfoldment. Through these techniques one can achieve an insight into areas where difficulties might emerge, and see how they can be dealt with and harmonized if they do. Areas of a relationship where particularly strong consolidations of energy and experience might be formed can also be observed by synastric means.

THE LANGUAGE OF SYNASTRY

Since astrology reduces all functional and experiential activities into a few essential symbols, in its most inclusive applications it can be used to explore the complex webs of relationship between anything and everything else. Astrology is a system of universal symbolism; its techniques apply holistic perception to the dynamic relationships existing between and within all organic wholes for the purpose of revealing a universal or a particular truth.

Symbols can be seen as archetypes that have significance on any number of levels. Natal astrology generally deciphers these symbols in terms of the life experiences and unfoldment of individuals as distinct entities—essentially on the level of selfhood. Synastric astrology relies on and overlaps natal techniques to a large extent, deciphering the same symbols on a different level, the level of relatedness.

As a symbol of *selfhood*, Mars, for instance, can be deciphered as actional energy and the capacity of an individual to move outward from his own center, to go out into the world and make an impression on it. On the level of *relationship*, Mars stands for, among other things, the capacity of an individual (or a couple or a group or individuals) to initiate collective experiences and act together with others for the achievement of an outer purpose. The polar opposite of Mars is Venus, the planet symbolizing, on the level of *selfhood*, the urge toward inner communion, the sense of appreciation, aesthetics, and values. In terms of *relatedness*, Venus stands for the capacity of individuals to appreciate and be receptive to one another and to participate in mutual experiences that express their personal, inner values, ideals, and aesthetics in a harmonious manner.

THE BIRTH CHART AS A "SEED PATTERN"

In synastry the chart of one person is compared with the chart of another person, or with the chart of a country, an enterprise, an occasion, or some other entity. Anything that has come into being has a beginning, and therefore its birth chart can be calculated. Although synastry is primarily used for the consideration of interpersonal relationships, our relationships with cities, man-made objects, businesses, animals, ideas, and even problems or crises can be studied with synastric techniques.

The foundation of synastry lies in the understanding of birth charts from the individual as well as the combined perspective. If the astrologer does not understand two persons as individuals, he will not be able to understand their relationship. In the same way, a person who is not in harmony with his or her own self will encounter difficulties in maintaining harmonious relationships with others.

The first step in chart comparisons, then, is to come to a clear understanding of what a birth chart essentially represents as a symbol of selfhood and to achieve a working familiarity with all the elements that compose it.

A birth chart is a graphic representation of the positions of the planets (including the sun and the moon) viewed from the particular place and time of one's emergence into independent existence. It represents the archetypal pattern of selfhood, describing this pattern in terms of both essential being and the process of becoming. A birth chart can be seen as the answer to the need of a particular time—the need of the universe for a particular kind of individual as well as the need of the incarnating entity for a particular quality of being, best suited to further the evolutionary process. No chart is, then, superior or inferior to any other, but is "best" for the accomplishment of a specific purpose. In *The Astrological Houses* (Doubleday, 1972), Dane Rudhyar aptly describes the significance of the birth chart as a

> formula structurally defining a man's "fundamental nature." It is a complex cosmic symbol—a word or *logos* revealing what the person is potentially. It is the individual person's "celestial name," and also a *set of instructions* on how a person can best actualize what at his birth was only pure potential—"seed potentiality." The birth chart is a *mandala*, a means to achieve an all-inclusive integration of the personality. [p. 20]

THE COMPONENTS OF THE BIRTH CHART

A chart should be initially viewed as a whole, as a gestalt, then studied in terms of its individual parts (described below), and then perceived once more as a whole composed of those interacting processes and parts. The parts include the following:

1. *The cross of the horizon-meridian* composed of two lines that divide the space surrounding the time and place of birth into four quadrants. Because the terrestrial equator and the ecliptic intersect one another rather than being parallel, an astrological chart is seldom composed of four equal quadrants when projected upon the background of the zodiac. That is, two opposite quadrants usually span more zodiacal degrees than the other two—even though they represent equal amounts of space surrounding the birth.[2]

The *horizon* (see Figure 9) is the horizontal line extending from the eastern horizon (the *ascendant*—symbolic of individuality and the self) to the western horizon (the *descendant*—representing relatedness and the other) at the time and place of birth. When this axis is extended into space it can be correlated to two opposing degrees of the zodiac. The *meridian* is a vertical axis that is drawn perpendicular to the horizon. It connects the two points of solar culmination: the M.C. (Medium Coeli), the symbolic noon point; and the I.C. (Imum Coeli), the midnight point. The meridian represents a line of individual growth (I.C.) and power or purpose (M.C.).

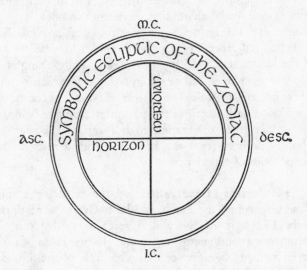

Figure 9

The four poles of the horizon-meridian axes are often called the "angles" of the chart. These four cardinal points define the chart's basic structure. Determining the zodiacal degrees of the angles is the initial step in casting an astrological chart.[3]

Because the Earth rotates a complete turn on its axis every day, the zodiacal degree rising (on the ascendant) changes rather rapidly —every degree of the zodiac appears on the horizon once every day, for approximately four minutes.

2. *The circle of twelve houses*, numbered in a counterclockwise direction beginning with the ascendant (see Figure 10). The twelve houses are derived through a threefold division of the space between the four angles. There are several methods of house division —based on slightly different procedures and resulting in somewhat different intermediary house cusps (cusps are the lines that mark the end of one house and the beginning of another). All house-division systems start with the same angles: the ascendant, I.C., descendant, and M.C. which are, respectively, the first, fourth, seventh, and tenth house cusps. The Porphyry system of house division, that simply divides the number of zodiacal degrees within each quadrant into thirds, is used in the charts that appear in this book.

The angles and the houses are the astrological symbols for the most individualized aspects of a person. This is because the framework of the houses is derived from the most rapidly changing of all cycles usually employed in astrology, the daily rotation of the Earth. The horizon-meridian represents the axes, or cross, of individual selfhood and describes the person as a unique being, signifying his or her basic orientation to self and to the world. The twelve houses derived from the horizon-meridian refer to twelve fundamental fields of experience.

3. The 360 degrees of *the ecliptic of the zodiac*, the apparent path of the sun around the Earth, and its twelve signs of thirty degrees each. The signs of the zodiac refer to twelve qualities of human temperament and energy utilization—having more of a collective (less individual) significance than the circle of the houses insomuch as the signs are derived from the longer, more collective cycle of the yearly revolution of the Earth around the sun.

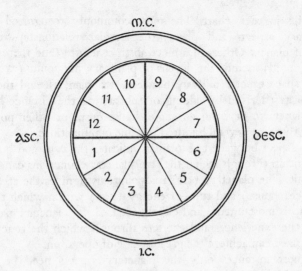

Figure 10

Every planet—or any celestial object, for that matter, from man-made satellites to galaxies—has a longitudinal position between 0°00′ to 359°59′ ahead of the beginning of the ecliptic (the vernal equinox). When the sun and Mars are conjunct at ten degrees Aries, if one extends a line of longitude from the center of the Earth through the sun straight to the limits of our solar system, then the center of the planet Mars will make contact with this line on a "vertical" plane—though the two bodies might not be on the same latitude, or "horizontal" plane. Since the zodiacal degree is ten Aries, we know that this conjunction occurs at a point in the zodiac exactly ten degrees past the point the sun occupied on the vernal equinox.

4. *The planets* placed within the houses in terms of their zodiacal positions. The planets are the basic variables of astrology and are viewed in the framework provided by the zodiac and the houses. They signify ten basic functions or processes found in all forms of organic life.

5. *The relationships* existing between all the planets and between the planets and the angles. There are numerous of these subtle rela-

tionships in each chart. The most commonly recognized are the planetary aspects and phases—the angular relationships between pairs of planets. Others of a more abstract nature (and therefore not widely used) include the dozens of planetary midpoints (axes of zodiacal space exactly midway between two planets), and the planetary parts (derived by adding or subtracting the distance between two planets to or from an angle, house cusp, or other point), of which there are several hundred possible combinations.

The aspect between two planets indicates the type and quality of relationship through which the two planetary functions can best act as a unit. The planetary pair's midpoint axis signifies the area of experience (house) and type of energy (sign) within which the relationship is most intense and clearly focused. Its planetary parts represent the experiences and energies through which the functions so synthesized can achieve the greatest ease of operation.

In most instances only the planetary aspects need be closely studied. Midpoints, parts, and phase angles can be extremely valuable when a closer look at a chart, or a planetary pair, is desired.

In the following pages we will explore the essential nature of the astrological frames of reference, as well as their significance in terms of synastry. First we will discuss the function of the planets, then the planetary aspects and their phases, the angles and the twelve houses, and the zodiac of signs.

The planets are symbols for ten essential functions that compose, in varying degrees, all forms of organic life. A planet's function is always essentially the same. It operates in terms of an individual (whether an individual person, relationship, nation, etc.) according to its house position, its sign, and its relationships with all the other planets in the chart. The house signifies the field of experience through which the planetary function can best express itself. The sign occupied by the planet symbolizes the type of energy best suited to project the planet through the experience. The planet's relation to all other bodies within the same chart indicates how it can best participate in a well-balanced development of the whole individual.

NOTES

1. Thorough descriptions and interpretations of the ecliptic and other astrological frames of reference are included in the following chapters.

2. The question of house division is one of the most complicated and controversial areas of astrology. A detailed account can be found in Dona Marie Lorenz' *The Houses* (Topanga, California: Eomega Press, 1974).

3. *A Handbook for the Humanistic Astrologer* (Garden City: Anchor Press/Doubleday, 1974) includes very thorough instructions for casting an astrological chart as well as a review of the various tools the process requires.

A number of firms now offer computer calculated astrological charts, providing an alternative to those who are interested in astrology but are reluctant to do the necessary calculations themselves.

4. THE PLANETS

Astrology is the study of the relationship that has been observed to exist between the cyclic motions of celestial bodies (particularly the sun, moon, and planets) and life on Earth. As we will see in the following chapters, there are many ways to approach the consideration of this relationship; astrologers use different frames of reference in investigating the infinitely complex symbolic language of the universe. The positions of the planets, for instance, can be considered in the structure of either the tropical zodiac (of signs) or the sidereal zodiac (of the constellations), and there is a choice of at least nine methods for dividing the birth chart into houses. All astrologers do agree, however, that planetary motions and cycles are at the foundation of any system of astrology.

CYCLES AND THEIR PHASES

The investigation of the cyclic motions of the celestial bodies can be simplified as well as expanded by using the concept of *phase*. A phase is the span of space and/or time between significant points in the internal structure of any whole cycle. Once a given segment of space or time can be described as a cycle, it can be divided by various numbers into successive phases. Planetary aspects mark the beginnings and ends of some of these phases, being experienced as recognizable turning points in an unfolding cycle, directing or redirecting the flow of one's experiences along the path of fulfillment.

The most apparent of a cycle's turning points are those derived by the divisions of two and four, experienced on the collective level, for example, in the cycle of day-night (based on the diurnal rotation of the Earth) and in the cycle of the four seasons, the environmental changes that accompany the comings and goings of the equinoxes and solstices (a result of the yearly revolution of the Earth around the sun).

Three hundred-sixty is, of course, the number associated with any complete cycle/circle, derived from the relationship between the day and the year. The fact that the *archetypal* pattern of 360 doesn't quite match the *actual* cycle of 365.26 days per year is an interesting point. In *An Astrological Mandala* Dane Rudhyar says:

> It is true that the year contains more than 360 days, which means that the earth rotates more than 360 times around its polar axis during a complete revolution around its orbit; but an intriguing feature common to all celestial periods is that they can never be measured in whole numbers and no planetary cycle is an exact multiple of another . . . The 360-degree zodiac is a *formula of archetypal relationships;* but our human experience presents to our consciousness a slightly larger sequence of days and nights. The 360-degree cycle refers to *the meaning* of experience; the day-night sequence to *the facts* of experience. [p. 16]

The word "phase" has been used in astrology most frequently to describe the regular successive appearances of the moon—a result of the constantly changing relationship between the sun and the moon from the viewpoint of the Earth. Here we have a very distinct and visible fourfold structure: the new moon (the invisible phase, when the unilluminated side of the moon is facing the Earth); the first-quarter moon (with its west side illuminated and its east side left in the dark); the fully illuminated full moon; and the third-quarter moon (opposite to the first-quarter moon).

Modern astrology, like the medieval and classical forms of astrology it is directly founded upon, has pretty much neglected, at least in practice if not in theory, the fact that almost every astrological frame of reference is fundamentally a cycle composed of phases. Astrologers who practice according to the traditional form tend to see the components of any astrological frame of reference (the cycle of the houses, the ecliptic of the zodiac, planetary aspects, etc.) as separate, isolated entities rather than as interdependent and interacting parts of a whole system. The meaning and nature of the zodiacal sign Virgo, for instance, is actually derived from the fact that it is the sixth sign (or phase) in a series of twelve, that it follows the fifth or self-expressive, creative sign Leo, and therefore symbolizes adjustments in consciousness needed by the self-expressive individual in order that he or she may engage in harmonious relations with others (symbolized by Libra, the seventh sign of the zodiac, whose beginning coincides with the fall equinox).

Traditional or classical astrologies are based on lateral thinking (even if they're actually dealing with cycles); humanistic or phase-oriented astrologies are founded upon a holistic, cyclic understanding of the ordered pattern of the growth and unfoldment of life. Life, on all levels, emerges and unfolds in a cyclic, spirallic manner for the achievement of a series of purposes. Through the study of astrology, a person can come to a clearer understanding of the meaning of life and discover how to go about understanding and fulfilling his or her spiritual potential at any given moment.

Of particular importance to the development of the ideas we intend to put forth in this and the following chapter is Marc Jones's study course on "Pythagorean Astrology" (dealing with the significance of numbers as the basis for the meaning of planetary aspects) and Rudhyar's *The Lunation Cycle* and *An Astrological Mandala*. In a more recent publication, *Phases of the Moon*, Marilyn Busteed, Richard Tiffany, and Dorothy Wergin take the basic ideas presented by Rudhyar in *The Lunation Cycle* concerning an eightfold division of the soli-lunar relationship one step further to a system of twenty-eight phases (about one phase for each day of the lunation cycle). The book includes much interpretive information from William Butler Yeats's *A Vision*. Although *The Lunation Cycle* and *Phases of the Moon* deal only with the soli-lunar relationship and exclusively with the eighth and twenty-eighth harmonics, this relationship can be used as a model for that between *any* two planets, and their cycles may be divided into more or less than eight phases, with distinct meanings correlating to each set of phases, derived from the particular number used as divisor.

All cycles, no matter how many phases they are divided into, can be seen archetypally according to what Rudhyar has called the "cyclic process." From a holistic, cyclic point of view the meaning of any individual astrological factor is inherent in and dependent upon first, the nature of the frame of reference (the process) as a whole—the nature of the whole cycle of houses, the zodiac of signs, the system of planets that revolve around our sun, etc.—and second, the sequence of the factor in consideration of the whole process, its relationship to the other individual parts of the same frame of reference. An astrological factor has meaning in that it is a part of a larger cyclic process.

The cyclic process outlined below can be applied to all astrological "wholes."

The *beginning* of the cyclic process is a moment of unity and oneness that immediately ceases to be a manifestation of external unity and becomes a process. This process is twofold: involutionary and evolutionary. The involutionary hemicycle succeeds the beginning, and here *life* is absorbed into *form* and *matter:* life becomes involved (brought into an intricate of complicated form or condition) in the building of organisms and structures and in the continual complexification and differentiation of individual structural patterns. This is the process of the One becoming the Many.

The *middle* is a point of repolarization, from the complexification of patterns to the creative release of their contents. This repolarization usually involves an increase of objective awareness accompanied by some sort of crisis (and the reorientation may not always be successfully accomplished). If the process of repolarization from the involutionary to the evolutionary hemicycle is successful, there can be growth in understanding and consciousness. The evolutionary hemicycle embodies the process of dissemination and participation.

The *end* is the moment of in-gathering of the energies and fruits of the just completing cycle. It is a seed moment whan all that has been actualized during the cycle is brought into a highly condensed form that will provide the structural pattern for the next cycle, the next cycle beginning on a new level of experience and activity.

THE FUNCTIONS OF THE PLANETS

Each of the ten planets (including the sun and moon since they too appear to "wander" in the geocentric sky) symbolically functions within a specific role in the life of any individual, be it an individual person or an individual relationship. When we view our solar system as a whole we can easily understand the basic astrological meaning and function of each planet as it is derived from its serial place in the whole system—that is, in terms of its position relative to the light- and life-giving center, the sun, as well as its position relative to the Earth's orbit. The function we assign to Mercury is an expression of the fact that Mercury is the closest planet to the sun; Venus' meaning is derived from the fact that it is the second planet from the sun and the first within the orbit of the Earth, etc. The following is an attempt to describe the meanings and functions of each of the ten planets according to this "organic" view and with special attention given to each planet's significance in terms of relatedness and relationship.

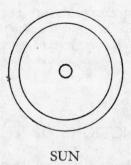

SUN

KEYNOTE: The central source of life energy that sustains, integrates, and gives purpose to individual existence.

Astronomical Characteristics: The sun is the center of our solar system as well as a star with its own special position in the galaxy. It is 864,000 miles in diameter and has a density that is only a fraction of the Earth's.

Abstract Meanings: The symbol for the sun is the circle of oneness and boundless potentiality with a point at its center, bringing solar potential to focus within individual consciousness. In *mythos* the sun is closely connected with the Father-Godhead images and, of course, with the sun gods: Ra to the Egyptians, Surya to the Hindus, and Helios to the Greeks.

The seed essence in which all processes have their beginning and end is symbolized by the sun as well as the energy that vitalizes and propels the consciousness through the myriad of forms it adapts in the evolutionary process.

Synastric Meanings: The central purpose of an individual to which all contacts and experiences are ultimately related. The energy that vitalizes and sustains any particular realtionship so that it can achieve its purpose. Traditionally, the sun is associated with the images of mature men and the "husband." It can also be seen as the archetype of masculine energy operating through universal will.

MOON

KEYNOTE: The reflective principle that protects and nourishes individuals along the path of growth and actualization of solar potential.

Astronomical Characteristics: The moon is the Earth's natural satellite, orbiting around us at a distance of about 239,000 miles, about 92 million miles from the sun. It takes an average of 27.32 days for the moon to complete one zodiacal (or sidereal) cycle and 29.53 days to complete a synodic cycle (from new moon to new moon).

Abstract Meanings: The arc or crescent symbol for the moon represents the principle of receptivity, the vessel that absorbs or the lens that focuses solar power, transmitting it to Earth. The moon is intimately associated with the mother principle, and is, according to occult philosophy, the "mother" of the earth.

The moon symbolizes the matrix from which the solar seed emerges in organic form. It is also the seventh, synthetic principle that mediates between or integrates the personal realm of the sun, Mercury, and Venus with the social realm of Mars, Jupiter, and Saturn.

Synastric Meanings: The feelings and instincts that enable us to be sensitive and emotionally receptive to others. The moon is the adjusting principle that nourishes a relationship and enables the individuals it unifies to adapt to one another's needs. Mature women and the "wife" are said to be connected with the moon as well as the archetype of feminine, receptive energy as it functions on the level of universal love.

MERCURY

KEYNOTE: *The mind engaged in perceiving and communicating.*

Astronomical Characteristics: The orbit of Mercury is 36 million miles from the sun; it takes Mercury 88 Earth days to complete one revolution. Because Mercury occupies a position in the solar system nearer to the sun than to Earth it can never be more than twenty-eight zodiacal degrees from the sun, geocentrically. Mercury is the smallest, hottest, and fastest (in linear velocity) planet of our solar system.

Abstract Meanings: The symbol of Mercury is a synthesis of the lunar crescent of receptivity, the circle of spiritual oneness, and the cross of matter. From a mythological perspective this symbol can also be seen as the caduceus of Hermes (Mercury to the Romans), signifying the creative, electric energies of nature (kundalini).

The initial phase in the process of differentiating the one solar power, bringing about the first stage of personalized duality, manifesting in the form of electrical, mental, and nervous energies is represented by Mercury.

Synastric Meanings: The mental and communicative functions that enable an individual to be aware of his or her own inner world as well as able to share and exchange experiences with others. The lines of communication within a relationship that allow the basic interchange of ideas and energies between two or more people. Traditionally, Mercury represents younger people, brothers and sisters. It is androgynous by nature—symbolizing the equal union of masculine and feminine energies.

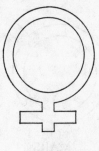

VENUS

KEYNOTE: *The centripetal element of experience that urges individuals toward achieving union with their inner self and with others.*

Astronomical Characteristics: Venus is the first planet inward from the Earth and has a diameter, volume, mass, gravity, and density very similar to that of the Earth. A unique feature of this planet is that its day (247 Earth days) is longer than its year (225 Earth days). Next to the sun and moon, Venus is the brightest object to be seen in the geocentric sky, and is never more than forty-seven zodiacal degrees from the sun.

Abstract Meanings: The glyph of Venus represents the circle of spirit placed over the cross of matter and is closely related to the Egyptian Ankh. In *mythos* the love goddesses of all peoples express the Venus principle.

Venus refers to the establishment of individual values and ideas that give inner meaning to personal existence. While Mercury represents the phenomenon of electrical energy, Venus symbolizes the phenomenon of magnetism and attraction-repulsion.

Synastric Meanings: The magnetic energies of relationship that draw individuals into contact with others. The values, ideals, and aesthetics of an individual and his or her appreciation of self and others. Young and/or particularly feminine women are represented by Venus traditionally, and it serves as an archetype for the personalized love principle.

MARS

KEYNOTE: The centrifugal forces of experience that urge individuals toward external expression and action for the concrete realization of solar potential as guided by Venusian visions and values.

Astronomical Characteristics: The first planet outward from the Earth, having an orbit 142 million miles from the sun, requiring 687 Earth days to complete. Mars has a diameter of only 4,200 miles and is well known for its reddish hue and network of "canals." It has two very small satellites of only five and ten miles in diameter.

Abstract Meanings: The symbol of Mars illustrates the function of spirit projecting itself through the vehicle of matter for the attainment of a definite goal upon which a value has been placed. The war gods of all *mythos* can be related to the Martian function of externalization.

Mars symbolizes the external, objective emergence of the solar potential (germination) and the initial development of an ego center capable of acting within and experiencing the social realm.

Synastric Meanings: One's capacity to externalize solar energy and initiate relationships. The active, expressive element of any relationship that urges individuals to act in harmony (or conflict). Mars is said to be representative of young and/or athletic men and is the archetype of the personalized will or power principle.

JUPITER

KEYNOTE: *The preserving principle that promotes the* status quo *of the established order along with its gradual expansion, and the assimilation of experiences within a well-defined area of activity.*

Astronomical Characteristics: The largest planet in our solar system, Jupiter is 483 million miles from the sun, having a rotational cycle of only ten Earth hours and a revolution of 11.86 Earth years. It is about 89,000 miles in diameter and has thirteen moons, four of which orbit the planet in a retrograde fashion.

Abstract Meanings: The lunar, receptive crescent functioning for the purpose of material expansion is suggested by Jupiter's astrological glyph. The function of expanding and preserving the Martian impulses is represented by Jupiter. It also symbolizes the vision and attainment of a larger, more inclusive philosophical and/or social horizon.

Synastric Meanings: The principles that promote the increase and preservation of any field of activity and relationship are symbolized by Jupiter. It also represents the social, moral, philosophical, and religious implications or pressures involved in an interpersonal relationship. Jupiter is traditionally representative of middle-aged people in powerful social, religious, or financial positions. Whereas Mercury symbolizes the student or *chela,* Jupiter represents the teacher or *guru.*

SATURN

KEYNOTE: The principle of limitation and definition that provides a sense of security and identity, making possible focused and structural activity.

Astronomical Characteristics: Saturn is the most distant planet in our solar system visible to the naked eye, having an orbit 886 million miles from the sun. It has a day of about 10½ Earth hours and a year that is equal to 29.46 Earth years. A unique feature is its system of rings, about 50,000 miles wide and 10 miles deep, orbiting the planet almost exactly on the plane of its equator.

Abstract Meanings: The symbol of Saturn is supposed to represent the sickle of Cronus. It is very similar to an inversion of Jupiter's glyph, signifying the cross of matter dominating the receptive crescent. Saturn represents the archetype of parental authority and collective conventions and limitations. An individual's acquisition of security, power, and identity within both personal and social spheres is a Saturnian function.

Synastric Meanings: Saturn symbolizes the innate form, function, and structure of an individual or collective being that naturally place certain restrictions upon its activities and relationships. The political, professional, and karmic implications or pressures connected with a relationship. Older people and the father are traditionally represented by Saturn, as well as people with antiquated ideas and those holding positions of ultimate authority.

URANUS

KEYNOTE: The drive to transcend conventionality ... order to participate consciously in transformative processes.

Astronomical Characteristics: The first of the planets known only in modern times is Uranus, discovered in 1781 by William Herschel with the aid of the telescope. Uranus is 1,783 million miles from the sun and takes 84 Earth years to complete one orbit. It has an extremely inclined polar axis, 98° to the plane of its orbit.

Abstract Meanings: The symbol for Uranus is of modern origin and could be interpreted as the unification of the principles of duality (the two vertical arcs) bringing about an ascent of spirit.

Uranus signifies the processes of change and transformation that eventually take us to a realm beyond the confines of Saturnian ego or social conventions, making possible an exploration of the further reaches of human consciousness.

Synastric Meanings: The element of experience that urges us to evolve and transform our relationships beyond the scope of Saturn's confines so that we may be able to realize a new dimension of togetherness. The unusual, unconventional, transformative aspects of relationship. The force that attracts individuals compulsively toward togetherness for transcendental reasons that may not be entirely evident or socially acceptable.

NEPTUNE

KEYNOTE: *The dissolution of antiquated forms and structures and the emergence of more inclusive, universal values and principles.*

Astronomical Characteristics: Neptune is about 30,000 miles in diameter, with an orbit 2,797 million miles from the sun and a period of 164.8 Earth years. It was discovered in 1846, its position calculated beforehand by astronomer-mathematicians who realized that certain eccentricities in the orbit of Uranus must be connected with the presence of another body beyond its orbit.

Abstract Meanings: The trident of the lord of the sea was naturally chosen as the glyph for Neptune. It represents the receptive trinity of human consciousness (sensual, emotional, and mental) brought in touch with the material realm, yet still reaching beyond it. Neptune is closely related to psychic experiences and the ability to transmit and receive transcendental experiences.

The dissolution of antiquated forms that have been shattered by Uranus is a Neptunian function. The psychic functions, especially when directed toward the realization of universal oneness.

Synastric Meanings: Neptune represents the drive toward reaching a state of total unity with another. It also symbolizes the function that leads individuals to oneness with nature through universal love. At the Neptune station, personalized love is not what is important, but the need to love and achieve oneness with all.

PLUTO

KEYNOTE: *The final stage in the process of transformation (that began with Uranus), bringing us to the threshold of a new cycle in the unfoldment of consciousness.*

Astronomical Characteristics: Pluto is the most remote planet in our solar system, having an orbit about 3,670 million miles from the sun and a period of about 264 Earth years. The most unique feature of this planet is the fact that, because of its extremely eccentric orbit, Pluto actually spends a part of its cycle within the orbit of Neptune. It is still unknown exactly when Pluto will next penetrate Neptune's orbit (symbolically announcing an acceleration of evolution within our solar system), but most astronomers calculate this event to occur in 1978.

Abstract Meanings: The symbol of Pluto, also of recent origin, can be seen as a seed of spiritual oneness contained within the crescent of receptivity over the cross of matter. Pluto not only is named after, but also carries the meaning of the Roman god Pluto, king of the underworld.

Rebirth through the regeneration of one's values, ideals, and pattern of being are symbolized by Pluto.

Synastric Meanings: The capacity of any relationship to emerge anew from the ashes of the past for the accomplishment of a great collective drama. The regenerative function of sex and relationship.

5. PLANETARY PHASES AND ASPECTS

Twenty-five hundred years ago the philosopher-mathematician Pythagoras taught that geometry and number were keys to the mysteries of the universe. Pythagoras discovered the arithmetic ratios underlying the diatonic scale of music, the construction of the regular geometric solids, the Pythagorean theorem, and he or perhaps one of his followers was one of the first to declare the sun to be the center of the solar system with the spherical planets (including the Earth) revolving around it. He also taught that every number has a special quality and meaning—and that underlying every existential fact there is a number or a series of numbers.

Astrology is essentially an application of the concept of the central and universal importance of number. The previous chapter introduced the idea that an individual astrological house, sign, or planet has its particular meaning because it is part of a whole cycle, occupying a specific position in the sequence of all the parts that comprise that cycle. Our example was the sign Virgo, which symbolizes the phase of reorientation in the entire zodiacal cycle of twelve signs (or phases): It is the sixth sign, falling just after the fifth, self-expressive, creative sign of Leo and immediately before the seventh sign of Libra, which begins at the halfway point of the zodiac at the transition from the subjective to the objective realms of consciousness. Likewise, the planet Venus symbolizes the function of inward evaluation and magnetism because it is the first planet inward from the Earth.

The significance of number can be found everywhere in astrology. In an article titled "Numerical Keys to Astrology" (*Horoscope*, April 1965), Rudhyar wrote:

> Number is the soul of Astrology, for it is the numerical sequence of the characteristic phases of such periodic motions (i.e., of planetary cycles) which is the basis of all astrological symbolism . . . Our universe is an ordered universe—a universe of processes whose many phases can be numbered. The number of each phase tells us what the phase basically signifies—this, with reference to the process as a whole. [p. 7]

While the Pythagoreans held that every number, from one to infinity, has its own particular significance, they demonstrated the numbers from one to ten to be the most primary and essential. The foundation of astrological interpretation and symbolism lies within the meaning and application of these numbers.

One, the monad, is the origin of all things, symbolizing unity and essential oneness. It is related to the sun and the conjunction aspect.

Two, the dyad, the first of the even numbers, signifies matter and the process of the involution or descent of spirit into matter. The dyad divides all things into two contrasting realms, a prerequisite for consciousness: subject-object, internal-external, self-other, etc. It represents the processes of externalization, division, and analysis. The planet Mercury and the opposition aspect are connected with the number two.

Three, the triad, is the first odd number (the monad combines both odd and even in a state of unity). It signifies spiritual evolution, or the ascent of spirit from matter. Three symbolizes the principles of synthesis following thesis and antithesis, as well as relationship, vision, and equilibrium. The triad corresponds to the planet Venus and the trine aspect.

Four, the tetrad, symbolizes concrete manifestation, the material world, and "solid power." It represents the process of the emergence of tangible forms and organic life. The moon (and the Earth) and the square aspect are related to the tetrad.

Five, the pentad, is the symbol of self-expression and creative activity. It is almost universally recognized as the archetype of humanity. The pentad can be connected with Mars and the quintile (72 degree) aspect.

Six, the hexad, represents the principle of harmony and productivity. Jupiter and the sextile aspect can be seen as expressions of the number six.

Seven, the heptad, is considered by almost all occult traditions as the most sacred of all numbers—the number of the cosmic evolutionary processes. It combines the qualities of three (the dialectic process active in all relationships) and four (concrete form and organic life). The number seven represents Saturn and the septile (51 degree and 26 minute) aspect.

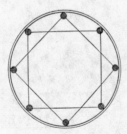

Eight, the ogdoad, symbolizes the power of willful individualism and dynamic activity. Uranus and the octile aspects (45 degree and 135 degrees) are related to the ogdoad.

Nine, the ennead, is, to the Pythagoreans, the ocean of fluid that surrounded all the lesser numbers and is itself contained by the decad. It symbolizes the final stages of the realization of an archetype and the threshold to a new realm of creative, cyclic activity. Nine can be seen as representing Neptune and the novile (40 degree) aspect.

Ten, the decad, represents the completion, or perfection, of the cyclic process that began with the monad, as well as being the starting point (monad) for a new cycle of activity on a higher level. Pluto and the decile (36 degree) aspect can be connected with the number ten.

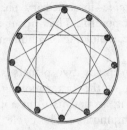

The number *twelve* occupies a significant place in all symbolical systems (including the Pythagorean) and is particularly fundamental in astrology. Twelve, the dodecad, is the number of the zodiacal signs and the houses. It is the result of the multiplication of three, the dialectic process—in astrology the three *modes* of activity and consciousness (cardinal, fixed, and mutable)—by four, the symbol of organic life and manifestation—represented by the four astrological *elements:* fire, earth, air, and water. The number twelve, then, is a synthesis of the trinity of consciousness or spirit with the cross of matter. It has a very meaningful role in the study of all forms of conscious, organic existence.

AN OUTLINE OF ASPECTUAL PRACTICES

All organic cycles of activity (the houses, the zodiac, the lunation cycle, etc.) are archetypically composed of 360 degrees. By dividing the 360 degrees by any one of many possible numbers, a cycle can be seen as a whole and, simultaneously, as a whole composed of interacting parts. The zodiac, for instance, is a 360-degree cycle divided into twelve phases, or signs, of 30 degrees each. In the article cited above, Rudhyar explains that astrology is

> a study of the meaning of cyclic series of facts (that is, *closed processes of transformation*). By "closed processes," I mean here processes which have a beginning and an end and

numerous—but *numerable*—intermediary phases. Such processes are also inherently purposeful. They occur to satisfy a "need," whether it be a cosmic, a biologic or a human need. [p. 8]

The relationship between any two planets is constantly changing, starting at conjunction, as the faster-moving planet moves away from the slower, traveling around its orbit and "catching up with" the other at the next conjunction. The cycle, from conjunction to conjunction, can be divided by 1, 2, 3, 4, 6, and 8 to arrive at what are called in modern astrology the "major" aspects (360 divided by 1 equals the conjunction; 360 divided by 2 equals 180, the opposition; 360 divided by 3 equals 120, the trine; 360 divided by 4 equals 90, the square, etc.). The "minor" or "abstract" aspects are a result of the divisions of 360 by 5, 7, 9 and 12. Each aspect represents a certain quality of relationship existing between two planets, symbolizing a particular sphere of individual consciousness.

The first aspects used by early astrologers were those emerging from a sense of time and the flux and flow of energies relative to time. The duality of day-night and the quadrature (four-partedness) of the cycle of the seasons are our direct experiences of a cycle divided by two and another by four. A line bisected by a perpendicular axis becomes a cross. The cross is an archetypal image found in all symbolical languages (in astrology: the axes of the equinoxes and solstices, the cross of the horizon-meridian, and the glyph for the planet Earth). A further division by two results in eight, an image of central importance in many oriental philosophies and appearing in the eight major phases of the moon as well as in the eightfold zodiacs and house structures that predate the modern twelvefold frame of reference.

As human intelligence began to develop more finely and was somewhat freed from the demands of the mundane activities of the material world, the twelvefold structure was introduced. It transcends, in many ways, the limitations of the strictly dualistic, polarized eightfold form. Probably when man's organic, biological functions were seen to operate in terms of the vibration of four, while his consciousness evolved in terms of three (thesis, antithesis, and synthesis; or subject, object, and the relationship between the two), the twelvefold phase cycle was developed as an appropriate framework. Thirty (360 divided by 12 equals 30) became a basic unit in astrological symbology.

From archaic times until the end of the sixteenth century astrologers used thirty almost exclusively as the basic unit in their recognition of aspects. The Ptolemaic aspects (conjunction, sextile, square, trine, and opposition), widely used from at least the first century A.D. to present times, are based on this tradition. They are the additive aspects produced by the successive *addition* of 30 plus 30 plus 30, etc.—only the semi-sextile (30 degrees) and the quincunx (150 degrees) are usually excluded, probably because they are considered "too weak" to be of importance.

Johann Kepler (1571–1630) felt that human consciousness was more evolved (at least among a few) and more attuned with a geometric order than could be described by the Ptolemaic aspects alone. To expand the arithmetic view, he introduced the divisive (or space-oriented) series of aspects, differing from the traditional *additive* aspects insomuch as they are geometric, that is, the result of the *division* of 360 by 1, 2, 3, 4, 5, 6, 7, and 8 (Kepler did not proceed beyond eight, with the exception of 12, though finer divisions are certainly valid). Kepler's new approach introduced three additional aspects to astrologers: the octile (45 degrees, having a supplement of 135 degrees), the quintile (72 degrees and the bi-quintile of 144 degrees), and the septile aspect (51 degrees and 26 minutes that can be multiplied by two and three, producing the bi-septile and the tri-septile). Until fairly recently Kepler's contribution has been pretty much neglected, and many astrologers still deal largely with the Ptolemaic or major aspects.

As is the case with most areas of astrological study, or any study for that matter, there are great differences of opinion about the practical importance of the aspects, as well as the degree or allowance of inexactitude (orb) to be used for various aspects. There are a few schools of thought that de-emphasize the role of aspects or employ only aspects of two and multiples of two (the conjunction-opposition, the semi-square or octile, the square, and the sesquiquadrate or tri-octile) because these aspects are considered the only ones directly related to events.

THE CYCLE OF PLANETARY ASPECTS

The significance of aspects (and the phases that exist between them) is an essential and initial study of phase interpretation.

The conjunction (o degrees) derives its meaning from the monad because it occurs when two planets occupy the same degree of the zodiac (although an orb of inexactitude of plus or minus about eight degrees is usually allowed in natal charts and about 3 degrees in synastric). It is based on the division by one, or no division at all, symbolically pointing to an essential unity operative between the two planetary bodies, as well as being the beginning of a new cycle of relationship.

The opposition (180 degrees) is the only aspect (when exact) in which the angular distance between the two planets is the same whether the phase arc is calculated in a clockwise or a counterclockwise direction. This aspect is connected with the basis of individual consciousness and identity. It is the fundamental aspect of duality, derived from the number two. It symbolizes the level of consciousness in which a basic distinction takes place between the inner and outer realms, and an equilibrium between subject and object, self and other, resulting in awareness, sensation, and sensitivity.

The static condition of the opposition does not remain unchanged. The two gives rise to the three, the opposition to the trine. While the conjunction and opposition (as well as all aspects evolving from successive divisions by two) are related to the sense of time, the trine (and all aspects based on *odd* numbers) is related to space and the principle of active intelligence.

The trine unites the duality of the opposition and gives to its factual type of consciousness the quality of intuition, and a vision of the purpose of existence. A relationship with another for the purpose of mutual transformation is an expression of this dynamic. The trine, being based on the division of a cycle by an odd number, is also connected with the evolution of the spiritual self—dealing more with intelligence and psycho-spiritual unfoldment than with natural, biological, and instinctual processes.

The vision and understanding of the trine, however, give rise to action, "purpose must carry the sword of decision," the three gives birth to the four. The square aspect (90 degrees) therefore symbolizes the mobilization of energies for the concrete actualization of the vision, ideal, and purpose of the trine. The trine is seen as the idea; the square represents a focused plan of action, the "architectural" aspect of growth and fulfillment.

What follows the vision of the trine and the plans of the square is the ability to *create*—the quintile (72 degree aspect). The quintile and the number five represent the human ability to manipulate substance in a creative and precise manner for the purpose symbolized by the trine and according to the design of the square. As we can all too easily see today, there are positive as well as negative uses of man's creative power. On one hand, we have the spiritual, creative power flowing through the individual or group for spiritual evolution—on individual, collective, and global scales—represented by a pentacle pointing up. In contrast is the presently widespread selfish and destructive use of technology and production for the furtherment of personal or group power, regardless of the consequences for others and for the planet as a living organism. The inverted, downward-pointing pentacle (also the emblem of black magic) is symbolic of this counter-evolutionary use of creativity.

In order to be truly constructive and creative in a spiritual manner, the quintile level of consciousness must be integrated with an understanding and vision of the results of its creative expressions and the way in which they can best fulfill an evolutionary need. In a series of articles written by Rudhyar about thirty years ago, titled "The Study of the Creative Process through the Less Familiar Aspects," he points out that

at the level of the quintile there is no real working relationship between creator and the public, leader and the led . . . But as the level of the sextile is reached by a sobered and more mature consciousness that has known creativeness for the sheer joy of creativity and found the experience wanting and perhaps tragic, the principle of cooperative creativeness begins to operate: creativeness integrated with understanding of the need and with consciousness of divine or universal purpose.

Since the symbol of the sextile (60 degrees) derives from two interlaced triangles, we can see that it is also related to an ability for solving problems posed by two contrasting types of understanding —and thus it represents the function of effective organization and management of one's energies.

The number seven produces the first irrational number when divided into 360—the septile aspect of 51 degrees 25 minutes and 42+ seconds—pointing to a new dimension of super-rational consciousness. The septile introduces the unpredictable, irrational element of experience, symbolizing the ability to respond to the call of one's destiny and to use unfit or left-over materials (more than six, but less than seven radii are required to make a circumference) for the purpose of fulfilling a definite goal, often of a karmic nature.

Next is the level of eight or the octile aspects (45 degrees and 135 degrees). If the square, from which the octile is derived, represents ideas and visions brought into a clear focus, then the octile symbolizes the dissemination of such ideas using the realm of one through seven as a foundation. The octile represents the dramatic and intense release of dynamic energy.

The aspects based on divisions of 360 by numbers greater than eight are connected with particularly abstract levels of human consciousness and functional activities. The novile aspect (40 degrees), based on the number nine, has been said to represent the identification of self with the purpose and function of global and universal schemes. The novile can also be seen as the symbol of initiation— emergence into a totally new realm.

The decile, or semi-quintile, of 36 degrees, can be symbolized by two interlacing pentacles (one pointed upward, the other, downward). It represents a point of conflict (or decision) between the positive and negative use of creative power—between a new creative impulse and old techniques and values.

The semi-sextile (30 degrees) and its supplement, the quincunx (150 degrees), result from the division of a cycle by twelve. The semi-sextile refers to the initial emergence of centers of individual consciousness. The quincunx (being the synthesis of twelve and five) refers to the principles of spontaneity and effective technique —as well as being a symbol of personal reorientation and self-improvement.

Waxing and Waning Hemispheres. In the cyclic process, every new cycle begins with the conjunction—the release of a new set of potentialities; culminates at the middle of the cycle—with the fulfillment of purpose on an *organic, functional* level, or the realization of failure; and ends, only to begin again on a new level, at the next conjunction. This process is a dynamic, spirallic cycle: Each new conjunction between two planets takes place at a slightly different point in space because both bodies are in constant motion. The structure may be repeated, but the experiences encountered and their reception are different for each cycle.

When we are dealing with an astrological chart we are working with a complex of relationships frozen in time—but still of a cyclic, dynamic nature. The conventional way of looking at aspects is to see them as "snapshots," but we should not forget that they are, in fact, moments of a continuous, endless process of cyclic change. All relationships are in constant motion. To view aspects from a phase orientation is to recognize this fact—a fact that implies an essential difference between waxing (from the conjunction to the opposition) and waning (from the opposition to the following conjunction) hemicycles of development. The nature of the aspect is constant regardless of whether it is waxing or waning, but its manifestation is modified according to its hemicycle.

The function of any aspect in the *waxing* hemicycle (with a phase arc between 0 degrees and 180 degrees) will be directed toward the development of potentials through the release of energies (generated by the planets involved) released along the path of impulsive and instinctual action. This is the arc of involution, differentiation and specialization.

The function of any aspect in the *waning* hemicycle (with a phase arc of 180 degrees to 0 degrees) should be directed toward the development and deepening of consciousness to the point where it can grasp the purpose of life (at least on certain levels) and disseminate it to others. This is the arc of mental activities and the expansion of consciousness.

Aspectual Orbs. Two planets do not have to be exactly the angular distance of an aspect apart to be considered in aspect. The number of degrees is the phase arc between two planets plus or minus the aspect value is referred to as an orb. For instance, a phase arc of eighty-eight degrees is a waxing square with a two-degree orb. Opinions among astrologers vary concerning the orb size they allow for the various aspects. An orb of about six to eight degrees is generally allowed for the major aspects (the conjunction, opposition, trine, and square) in natal charts. When working with synastric charts it is best to use narrower orbs, generally no more than three or four degrees, and preferably no more than two or three degrees. In addition to their value as parameters for determining aspects, orbs also have an underlying qualitative significance.

Applying and Separating Aspects. An applying aspect is one with a phase arc less than the exact aspect. As time progresses, the faster moving planet (the applying planet and the main releaser of the function of the planetary pair) will progress to a position making the aspect exact. An applying aspect is not yet mature, has not yet reached its apex of exactitude. A separating aspect is one in which the phase arc is greater than the aspect's arc. That is, the aspect has already culminated, and the faster moving planet is proceeding along a course that will lead it completely out of the orb of the aspect.

An applying aspect is one in which the planets' functions are directed toward the gradual increase and eventual release of activity, while a separating aspect represents the dispersion of the intensity generated and released in the applying stage.

In comparing two charts, if one's natal planet is forming an applying aspect with another's natal planet, within the field of activity symbolized by the two planets there should be a building of momentum and a drive toward fulfillment and release. In the instance of a separating aspect, a fulfillment in the particular function symbolized by the planets involved has already been realized. It is now up to the individuals to integrate its meaning into the fabric of their individualities and the relationship itself and move forward to the next phase of unfoldment. This next phase can be seen as the next aspect in the development of the cyclic relationship between the two planets.

The closeness of the orb indicates the intensity of the contact. The most exact aspect between the natal planets of two persons can symbolize the most immediate and intense area of interaction between the two individuals, the facet of the relationship that may be most in need of integration.

THE MEANING OF THE ASPECTS

The aspects symbolize basic types of interfunctional relationships defined by the planets that compose them. When interpreting planetary aspects it is important to consider not only the nature of the planets involved but also their positions in the zodiac of signs and the cycle of houses. These two frames of reference will be discussed further in the following chapters; they refer essentially to types of energy and fields of experience. The following is an attempt to briefly outline the significance of each aspect, with special focus on its meanings in synastry.

CONJUNCTION

Phase Arc: 0°
Numerical Value: 1

KEYNOTE: *The moment of unity setting the tone that will resonate throughout an entire cycle of relationship.*

Traditional Meanings: Togetherness, unity, intensification, and strength.

Symbolic Implications: The monad; the one primordial, eternal source. The point and the origin of all numbers.

Abstract Meanings: The release of a seed potential from which a new cycle of relationship will unfold. The synthesis and unity of two or more individual centers.

Synastric Meanings: The initial contact between two or more persons and the essential quality of that which their relationship potentially fulfills. A functional unity between two persons in the departments of life symbolized by the planets. The energies that draw individuals into intimate contact.

Types of Relationship: Total union. Contacts that resonate in the innermost recesses of the psyche. A conjunction between a planet in one natal chart and that of another represents the areas of life in which the individuals will be able to identify with one another.

OPPOSITION

Phase Arc: 180°
Numerical Value: 2

KEYNOTE: The line of distinction that maintains equilibrium between self and others.

Traditional Meanings: Tension, conflict, pulling apart, and separation.

Symbolic Implications: Duality. The two: above-below, light-dark, in-out, self-other, male-female. The line.

Abstract Meanings: The separation of subject and object and the subjective and objective modes of human consciousness. In cyclic terms, the integration of the subjective hemisphere with the objective, the confrontations, and new awareness such a process involves. The apex of any cycle of relationship.

Synastric Meanings: Interfunctional activity for the realization of one's inner self through contacts with others. The state of balance between self and other that precedes contact or interaction. Duality, the maximum separation of centers. Unity through diversity.

Types of Relationship: The opposition symbolizes the type of interactivity that may appear to be rooted in conflict on the surface, yet there is a complementary nature with an underlying sense of unity, and the opportunity for illumination. Planets in a synastric chart linked by opposition indicate the spheres of activity where the two individuals are most likely to have radically different views.

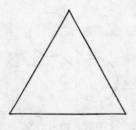

TRINE

Phase Arc: 120° and 240°
Numerical Value: 3

KEYNOTE: The harmonious blending of seemingly opposed functions through a mutual purpose or vision.

Traditional Meanings: Ease, harmony, flow, and co-operation.

Symbolic Implications: The trinity, the evolution of spirit, and the three modes of consciousness. The triad of will, love, and wisdom— the three aspects of the one in spirit.

Abstract Meanings: The transcendence of duality through understanding. The expansion of one's field of relationship and activity. WAXING: The expansion of the concrete mind; growth in terms of practical knowledge. WANING: The expansion of the abstract mind; growth in terms of universal understanding.

Synastric Meanings: The harmonious, co-operative interweaving of two or more individual life patterns. An understanding of others and their needs.

Types of Relationship: Harmonious, co-operative associations in which energies flow between centers without conflict, perhaps in a not altogether conscious manner.

SQUARE OR QUARTILE

Phase Arc: 90° and 270°
Numerical Value: 4

KEYNOTE: *The need to make definite plans for the actualization of an envisioned goal.*

Traditional Meanings: Difficulty, affliction, conflict, and stress.

Symbolic Implications: The four corners of the universe, the four seasons, and the four elements. The cross of matter through which the one is manifested.

Abstract Meanings: The process of externalizing relationship and the pursuit of giving to it concrete form. Creative tension. The need to meet confrontations directly. WAXING: Crises in action, encountered in answer to the need for the establishment of a firm base for externalization. WANING: Crises in consciousness, encountered in the development of new forms of relationships.

Synastric Meanings: The square symbolizes an interplanetary relationship in which there lies much constructive potential, probably realized through some conflict or stress.

Types of Relationship: Contacts that tend to be alternately stimulating and exciting, then tense and stressful. Once the surface conflicts implied by a square aspect is harmonized or integrated, a very constructive and purposeful relationship may emerge.

QUINTILE

Phase Arc: 72° and 288°
Numerical Value: 5

KEYNOTE: The capacity for creative manipulation of energies and substances for the actual manifestation of visions and plans.

Traditional Meanings: The quintile is rarely used by traditional astrologers. It is usually considered an indication of artistic talent.

Symbolic Implications: The five senses, the five limbs (two arms, two legs, and the head), the four fingers and the thumb.

Abstract Meanings: The individual, creative element active within any life experience. The ability to express one's inner self through artistry. Technology as a means of carrying out a definite plan of action in the creation of a product. WAXING: The use of knowledge and skill for the realization of a subjective or personal vision. WANING: Channeling one's understanding and creative abilities toward the realization of an objective or social/collective need.

Synastric Meanings: The quintile (as well as the bi-quintile aspect with an angular value of 144° or 216°) indicates the area of activity where two individuals should be able to interact on the level of creative expression.

Types of Relationship: Creative, artistic associations or those that bring individual and creative factors into focus.

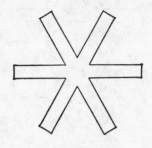

SEXTILE

Phase Arc: 60° and 300°
Numerical Value: 6

KEYNOTE: Creativity synthesized with a sensitive understanding of the needs and results of one's creations for one's self and others.

Traditional Meanings: Harmony, good, ease, a weak trine.

Symbolic Implications: The six directions of motion: up, down, forward, backward, left, right. Two interlaced triangles representing the union of two triads of self.

Abstract Meanings: The harmonious interlinking of two independent, yet complementary, fields of activity. The practical application of creativity, skills, and techniques. WAXING: The instinctual, spontaneous development of knowledge and skills. WANING: The purposeful application of techniques and understanding.

Synastric Meanings: Indicates the departments of life (symbolized by the planets involved) where two individuals can work together in a harmonious and productive fashion.

Types of Relationship: The sextile signifies an association in which individuals can combine their interests, skills, and understanding in a mutually gratifying manner for the ultimate purpose of furthering the evolution of humanity.

SEPTILE

Phase Arc: 51°26' and 308°34'
Numerical Value: 7

KEYNOTE: *The connections that link ordinary life experiences with transcendental needs.*

Traditional Meanings: Rarely employed by traditional astrologers; generally described as an indication of fate.

Symbolic Meanings: The cosmos. The seven visible planets and the seven days of the week. The seven cosmic rays.

Abstract Meanings: The unexpected, irrational, and transcendental elements of life. The karmic, collective, and cosmic implications of any field of activity. Destiny or the chain of experiences and relationships that leads one to his or her individual unfoldment. WAXING: An instinctual and spontaneous receptivity to the call of one's destiny. WANING: The use of intuition and understanding as a means of envisioning and achieving the fulfillment of one's destiny.

Synastric Meanings: A septile (as well as a bi-septile of 102°52' or 257°08' and a tri-septile of 154°17' or 205°43') aspect between two planets in a synastric chart indicates that the departments of life symbolized by the planets' functions may tend to become the stage for unusual and unexpected experiences, possibly of a spiritual or transformative significance.

Types of Relationship: Unions in which individuals are mysteriously, compulsively, or karmically drawn together.

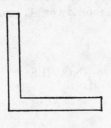

OCTILE

Phase Arc: 45° and 315°
Numerical Value: 8

KEYNOTE: The apex of interfunctional activity culminating in a dramatic and intense release of dynamic energies.

Traditional Meanings: Difficulty, affliction, a weak square.

Symbolic Implications: The apex of electromagnetic fields. Two interlaced squares.

Abstract Meanings: Intense interaction. The urge toward dynamic self-expression and the promotion of one's ideas. WAXING: An awareness of dynamic interactivity. WANING: The release of self through creative interchange.

Synastric Meanings: The intense interchange of personal energies. The planets linked by an octile (or tri-octile of 135° or 225°) denote the field of relationship that should allow for a maximum release of individual expression and bi-polar activity.

Types of Relationship: Powerful connections with others that could manifest either in an exciting and constructive or conflicting and difficult way.

NOVILE

Phase Arc: 40° and 320°
Numerical Value: 9

KEYNOTE: *The closing phase of a tenfold cycle of relationship that brings one to the threshold of a new realm of consciousness and relatedness.*

Symbolic Implications: The triads of mineral, plant, and animal kingdoms. The three facets of each of the aspects of the trinity. The forty days and nights of preparation for initiation.

DECILE

Phase Arc: 36° and 324°
Numerical Value: 10

KEYNOTE: *The integration of a new creative impulse and set of potentials, retaining the most suitable forms, techniques, and values of the past.*

Symbolic Implications: The Tetractys. The four universal beings manifesting as the numbers one, two, three, and four.

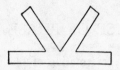

DUODECILE OR SEMI-SEXTILE

Phase Arc: 30° and 330°
Numerical Value: 12

KEYNOTE: *The emergence of a focal center of self-awareness.*

Traditional Meanings: Slightly good, not of much influence.

Symbolic Implications: The twelve solar archetypes. The twelve gates of the holy city. The twelve tribes of Israel.

Abstract Meanings: The most intimate linking of functional centers. WAXING: The beginning of an individualized center of consciousness. WANING: The final phase of a cyclic process where individual consciousness commences its return to a state of universalization.

Synastric Meanings: The duodecile aspect in a synastric chart indicates the area of a relationship in which the two individuals will feel naturally intimate.

The quincunx or quinduodecile (also known as the inconjunct) aspect of 150° or 210° is the supplement of the duodecile. It falls halfway between the harmonious trine and the tense opposition, signifying a phase in the development of a cycle where adjustment and reorientation should occur. A quincunx in a synastric chart indicates a strong sense of attraction-repulsion in the departments of life indicated by the planets forming the aspect.

Types of Relationship: A semi-sextile or quincunx aspect between two planets denotes a functional relationship that may alternate between intimacy and alienation.

THE USE OF PHASE ARCS

In a more thorough representation of planetary motion, not only all the angular values recognized by Ptolemy and Kepler, but *every* phase arc existing between any two planetary bodies (or between angles and planets) has a particular significance, whether or not an aspect is formed. Some of these relationships may be much more subtle than others, possibly working along the lines of a superphysical evolution, but operating on some level of consciousness, nevertheless.

Arriving at the meanings for any of these relationships is not difficult—particularly if one keeps in mind the two things that are at the foundation of phase interpretation:

(1) the *phase arc* (or the distance between two bodies calculated in a manner described at the end of this chapter) has a specific numerical value that can be deciphered in a number of ways, and

(2) the nature and function of the planetary relationship involved (represented by a synthesis of the two planets' functions, as well as by their positions in terms of house, sign, etc.) expresses itself according to the position of their phase arc within the context of their whole cycle.

We discuss ways in which to decipher the meanings of various planetary pairs in Chapter 6. The phase arc of any two planets can be interpreted either through the aspects presented above or in terms of the Sabian symbols, discussed in Chapter 7.

HOW TO CALCULATE PHASE ARCS

A natal phase arc is (except in the case of relationships between the sun, Mercury, and Venus) the distance between two planets measured from the slower-moving planet to the faster in a counterclockwise direction. For these calculations the moon is the fastest moving planet, followed by Mercury, Venus, sun, Mars, Jupiter, Saturn, Uranus, Neptune, and Pluto. There are forty-five combinations of planets. Phase arcs can be calculated by converting the zodiacal longitudes to their value in terms of a cycle of 360 degrees, then subtracting the slower-moving planet's position from that of the faster.

For example: 260°35'   (20°35' Sagittarius) Mars
              —110°05'   (20°05' Cancer) Jupiter
              ─────────
              150°30'   Mars-Jupiter phase arc

If the position of the faster moving planet is less than the slower, then 360 degrees should be added to its value.

For example: 20°10'   (20°10' Aries) Venus
              +360°00' Adjustment
              ─────────
              380°10'
              —255°05' (15°05' Sagittarius) Saturn
              ─────────
              125°05'   Saturn-Venus phase arc

The method of calculating synastric phase arcs between the planets of two persons differs: The distance is always taken from the older person's natal planets to the younger's in a counterclockwise direction.

The phase arcs between the sun, Mercury, and Venus are distinct from the others because these three bodies lie inside the orbit of the Earth. They are never more than a fraction of the zodiac apart from one another and therefore do not form geocentric oppositions that would mark the obvious transition from the waxing to the waning hemicycle. The phase arcs of these three combinations can be understood as waxing and waning, however, if we analyze the retrograde periods of Mercury and Venus.

Mercury and Venus spend half their cycles between the sun and Earth and the remaining time beyond the sun (see Figure 11). When one of these planets forms a conjunction with the sun while it is moving retrograde (and passing between the Earth and the sun), it is referred to as an inferior conjunction. A superior conjunction is formed when the planet is moving in a direct fashion and therefore beyond the sun from a geocentric perspective. A phase arc between the sun and the planets Mercury and Venus is *waxing* when (1) the planet (Mercury or Venus) is moving in a direct motion, is ahead of the sun in the zodiac, and is moving away from the sun after the superior conjunction—this is the *superior/waxing* phase, or (2) when the planet is retrograde and, behind the sun in the

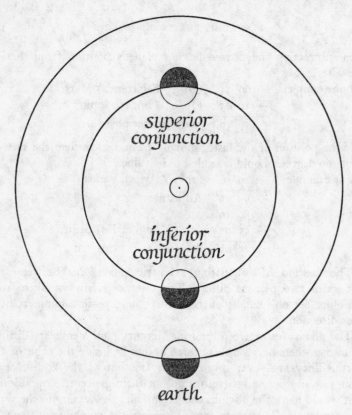

superior
conjunction

inferior
conjunction

earth

Figure 11

zodiac, is moving away from it after the inferior conjunction—this is the *inferior/waxing* phase. A *waning* phase arc between the planets Mercury or Venus and the sun occurs when (1) the planet is moving in a direct motion, behind the sun in the zodiac, and moving toward superior conjunction—this is the *superior/waning* phase, or (2) the planet is moving in a retrograde motion, ahead of the sun, and, because of its retrograde motion, moving toward the inferior conjunction with the sun—this is the *inferior/waning* phase.

In the instance of the phase arc between Mercury and Venus, the procedure is the same as above except that the position of Mercury is used instead of the sun's.

6. THE HOUSES

The most particularized frame of reference against which the planets can be viewed is the horizon-meridian and the twelve houses derived from the quadrants produced by these axes. The horizon and meridian divide the space surrounding the birth of an individual (or any event) into four segments equal in space. The horizon is composed of two poles or angles, the ascendant that expresses the degree of the zodiac at the eastern horizon at a particular time and place, and the descendant that relates the opposite zodiacal degree with the western horizon. Because the Earth rotates on its axis once every twenty-four hours, a different zodiacal degree rises (as its opposite sets) on the horizon about every four minutes (24 hours divided by 360 degrees equals four minutes). (See Figure 9 in Chapter 3.) Perpendicular in space to the horizon is the meridian, though it is not always ninety zodiacal degrees from the horizon, with the M.C. or Medium Coeli at its upper pole representing the point of solar culmination (the symbolic noon point) and the I.C. or Imum Coeli at its lower pole, the midnight point. The horizon represents a line of awareness that separates the subjective (lower hemisphere) and objective (upper hemisphere) modes of consciousness. The meridian signifies the line of organic growth (I.C.) and social power (M.C.).

The ascendant of an astrological chart symbolizes the qualities that make an individual (an individual person or an individual situation or relationship) unique. It is the selfhood pole of awareness and represents the type of experiences that can lead one to a more intimate understanding of his or her particular potentialities and their fulfillment. The ascendant symbolizes what an individual essentially is.

The descendant is always the zodiacal degree directly opposite (180 degrees from) the ascendant and symbolizes the individual's approach or orientation toward others. It is the relatedness pole of the line of awareness and represents where an individual's destiny should lead him, where a relationship should take its individual participants.

The I.C., popularly known as the "nadir," symbolizes the experiences that can best assist one in establishing a center of personal integration and roots for upward growth. How a relationship can be best grounded and how best approached by the individuals who compose it are represented by the I.C. as well.

The M.C., often incorrectly referred to as the "midheaven", signifies an individual's place and function on a collective, spiritual level, or his or her relation to the universe. It signifies the ultimate why of an individual self or relationship: why an individual is born or why two or more persons are drawn together in a relationship.

The areas between the angles are known as quadrants, each carrying an individual significance. The first quadrant is the area between the ascendant and the I.C. It signifies the initial emergence of self-conscious activity. The second quadrant, extending from the I.C. to the descendant, symbolizes the phase of most rapid organic growth and adaption as well as the expansion of awareness of the outer world, but from an essentially subjective perspective. The third quadrant extends from the descendant to the M.C. It represents the growing awareness of the outer world from an objective point of view and the creative release of self through interpersonal relationships. The fourth quadrant, from the M.C. to the ascendant, signifies the expansion of one's social/spiritual power and responsibility.

HOUSE DIVISION

The twelve houses of an astrological chart are produced by dividing the quadrants by three. In order to perform such a division, a choice must be made among the many valid systems of house division. That is, there is more than one way of dividing the space (or time, in terms of one system) within each quadrant. Each of the many systems emphasizes a certain astronomical framework. One system, for instance, focuses on the ecliptic, another on the equator, and so on. The four angles remain the same in all systems of division (with the exception of the equal house system that doesn't consider the meridian when dividing houses), but different systems assign varying degrees to the intermediary house cusps (the second, third, fifth, sixth, eighth, ninth, eleventh, and twelfth houses). The principles behind the various systems are too complex to present here; those interested are referred to *Tools of Astrology: Houses* by Dona Marie Lorenz (Topanga, Calif.: Eomega Press, 1973). The Porphyry system was used for the charts in this volume, a system that simply divides the zodiacal space within each quadrant into three segments equal in zodiacal space.

Why twelve houses? Astrology is an application of numerology; the symbolism of astrology becomes clear viewed from a numerological perspective. The houses are derived by a threefold division of the quadrants. This operation involves dividing *four* segments, symbolic of form and concrete manifestation, by *three,* signifying the three aspects of spirit or the three modes of consciousness that animate all forms of manifestation (four). The result is twelve archetypes, each expressing a particular aspect of the synthesis of the triangle of spirit with the cross of matter. In other numerological operations twelve represents three ($1+2=3$) and also the sacred number seven, symbolizing the cyclo-cosmic process ($3+4=7$).

QUALITIES OF HOUSE EXPRESSION

The threefold division of the quadrants, in addition to establishing three houses within each quadrant, defines the area within the quadrant where each one of the three qualities of expression is most focused. That is, there are twelve houses, one carrying the significance of each of the three modes of expression in each quadrant. This again highlights the numbers three and four: The twelve houses are divided by three qualities of expression, each quality most active within a total of four houses.

The Active or Angular Quality. Houses following the angles (the first, fourth, seventh, and tenth) are referred to as active or angular. The quality of expression dominant within these houses is activating, initiating, and individualizing. It sets processes and relationships into motion, and symbolizes the areas of one's primary experiences. These four houses are *generative*.

The Reactive or Succedent Quality. The houses following the active houses (the second, fifth, eighth, and eleventh) are called reactive or succedent. These houses symbolize the responses to the actions first expressed by the active houses. They have creative significance, representing the expansion, focalization, and consolidation of the relationships and experiences initiated in the active houses. These houses are *concentrative*.

The Resultant or Cadent Quality. The resultant or cadent houses precede the angles (the third, sixth, ninth, and twelfth houses). These are universal and harmonizing, tending to fulfill or disintegrate the relationships and experiences initiated in the active houses and focused in the reactive houses. They are *dispersive*.

THE MEANING OF THE TWELVE HOUSES

The twelve houses symbolize twelve archetypal areas of individual experience and life circumstance. Like all other astrological frames of reference, the twelve houses as a whole compose a cycle consisting of a beginning, a middle, and an end; the complete cycle encompassing the entire circle of twelve houses, with each house deriving its meaning from its sequence in the cycle. Outlines of the various meanings for each of the twelve houses follow.

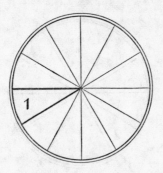

FIRST HOUSE

Expression: Active-angular/generative
Significators: Mars and Pluto

KEYNOTE: *The experience of emerging from the collective un-conscious as a self-conscious individual with a unique function to fulfill.*

Traditional Meanings: The circumstances one is born into. The personality and the body.

Abstract Meanings: The process of self-discovery, one's orientation toward one's self. The experiences through which one can best realize what he or she is. The most obvious characteristics projected by the personality.

Synastric Meanings: The direct and immediate significance of a relationship, how it could be affecting one's sense of self and identity. Experiences through which two or more persons can best participate together in mutual self discovery.

Types of Relationships: Contacts that originate on a self-to-self level or one's relationships with one's inner self.

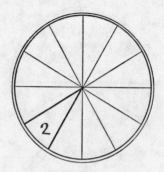

SECOND HOUSE

Expression: Reactive-succedent/concentrative
Significator: Venus

KEYNOTE: The experience of identifying one's self with sub-stance for the purpose of achieving a clearer definition of self.

Traditional Meanings: One's attitude toward possessions. Money and property.

Abstract Meanings: Experiences of identifying one's self with and becoming attached to substance. The refinement of the senses.

Synastric Meanings: The basic energies and resources latent within a particular relationship. How two or more individuals can co-operate on a practical level. The biological experiences of a rela-tionship. Two persons' approaches to sharing resources and ener-gies.

Types of Relationships: Biological contacts or relationships that deal extensively with materials and resources.

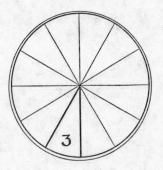

THIRD HOUSE

Expression: Resultant-cadent/dispersive
Significator: Mercury

KEYNOTE: *The establishment of a network of relationships between one's self and the environment. The acquisition of knowledge concerning one's environment.*

Traditional Meanings: The concrete mind, publications, writings, brothers and sisters, and short-term travel.

Abstract Meanings: The mental functions, sense impressions, and the associative faculties. Consciousness focusing itself upon the relationships between one's self and his or her environment.

Synastric Meanings: The experience of relating with others through the mental sphere. The communicative, verbal possibilities of a relationship. Experiences through which individuals can cooperate for the purpose of gathering knowledge and information. The manner in which two or more individuals can best communicate.

Types of Relationships: Relationships that are involved with the communication of knowledge. Contacts with one's siblings.

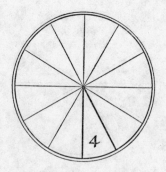

FOURTH HOUSE

Expression: Active-angular/generative
Significator: The moon

KEYNOTE: *The experience of forming a center of activity for the purpose of personal integration and inner security.*

Traditional Meanings: The home and the domestic scene. Physical and emotional security. The mother.

Abstract Meanings: Personal integration within a central, well-defined field of relationship. The process of integrating a part of one's environment within one's self for the purpose of establishing a center of outer experience.

Synastric Meanings: How a relationship influences one's personal foundations and one's sense of emotional security. How two or more persons can best go about sharing emotional experiences and a common base of operations.

Types of Relationships: Relationships centered around the home. Contacts with one's mother.

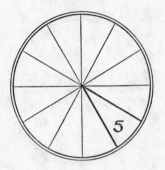

FIFTH HOUSE

Expression: Reactive-succedent/concentrative
Significator: The sun

KEYNOTE: *The process of externalizing one's self, and the experiences of self-expression as a vital, creative individual.*

Traditional Meanings: Casual relationships, pleasure, children, amusement, and speculation.

Abstract Meanings: The experience of externalizing one's self through creative expression. Individual and unique creative experiences one wishes to display to the world.

Synastric Meanings: The capacity for openly expressing one's emotions and affections. How two or more individuals can best co-operate on the level of self-expression and creativity. Collaboration with others on a creative project.

Types of Relationships: Casual love affairs that afford personal pleasure and spontaneous, creative expression without the responsibilities normally connected with contractual (seventh house) relationships.

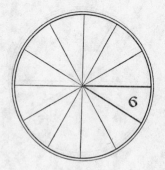

SIXTH HOUSE

Expression: Resultant-cadent/dispersive
Significator: Mercury

KEYNOTE: *The experience of resolving personal conflicts result-*
ing from overexpressing one's self (by way of fifth house experi-
ences) through introspection and self-reorientation.

Traditional Meanings: Health, employment, service to others, and
introspection.

Abstract Meanings: Personal limitations, inertia, and conflicts. Self-
judgment and analytic introspection as a means of dealing with personal inadequacies.

Synastric Meanings: The personal adjustments and reorientations
necessary for one to be able to relate to others in a harmonious
manner. Experiences of dealing with the conflicts that emerge in a
relationship on the issue of equality in personal expression and
authority. How two or more individuals can work together for the
purpose of mutual self-improvement and reorientation.

Types of Relationships: Contacts between employer and em-
ployee. Therapeutic relationships.

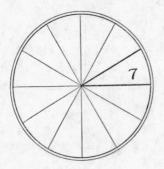

SEVENTH HOUSE

Expression: Active-angular/generative
Significator: Venus

KEYNOTE: *The process of objectifying consciousness, making possible experiences of one-to-one interchange that transcend the strictly subjective approach to relationships.*

Traditional Meanings: Marriage, partnership, contracts, and relationships in general.

Abstract Meanings: One's orientation toward others and toward relationship. Contractual relationships and agreements. The transition between subjective perception and active participation within the sphere of relationship.

Synastric Meanings: How two or more persons can best function together in a mutually co-operative fashion. The way in which one approaches relationships. The central focus of a relationship and where it could lead the individuals involved.

Types of Relationships: Conventional monogamous relationships are represented by the seventh house, as well as partnerships and other legally binding relationships.

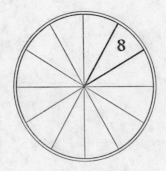

EIGHTH HOUSE

Expression: Succedent-reactive/concentrative
Significators: Mars and Pluto

KEYNOTE: The experience of an intense exchange of vital energies for the purpose of transcending individual limitations.

Traditional Meanings: Sex, death, business, the occult, and other people's money.

Abstract Meanings: The expansion of one's field of relationship. The mutual exchange of energies. Identification of self with a greater whole, "the urge to merge" with others while still retaining one's sense of individuality.

Synastric Meanings: The experience of interacting and identifying closely with another in both biological and spiritual spheres. A relationship's capacity for intense interplay between individuals. The experiences in which individuals can assist each other through personal transformations.

Types of Relationships: Business contracts and transactions. Intensely sexual and transformative relationships that transcend social demands and conventions.

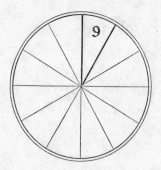

NINTH HOUSE

Expression: Resultant-cadent/dispersive
Significator: Jupiter

KEYNOTE: The experience of expanding one's social and philosophical horizons in order to reach a deeper understanding of the purpose of relationship.

Traditional Meanings: Religion, philosophy, and law. Journeys to foreign lands.

Abstract Meanings: The abstract mind and the power to recognize and understand multifaceted relationships. The expansion of consciousness and one's personal search for meaning.

Synastric Meanings: A relationship's ability to stimulate one's higher aspirations and expand one's world view. The experience of co-operating with others for the further understanding of the basic principles that underlie life.

Types of Relationships: Associations with others pursuing a common metaphysical line of inquiry. Relationships that involve the expansion of one's understanding possibly by bringing one into contact with different cultures and places.

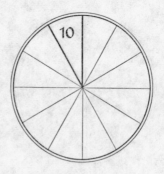

TENTH HOUSE

Expression: Active-angular/generative
Significator: Saturn

KEYNOTE: *The experience of participating in the outer world for the purpose of understanding and fulfilling one's collective/spiritual function.*

Traditional Meanings: Social status, recognition, honor, and ambition. The father.

Abstract Meanings: Active participation in the external, objective world. The place and function one holds in the social sphere, and the assumption of responsibility for its realization.

Synastric Meanings: The experience of working with others for a mutual social, political, or spiritual purpose. How an association can broaden one's understanding of his or her career or social position.

Types of Relationships: Contacts between individuals working for a common social goal. One's relationship with one's father or father images.

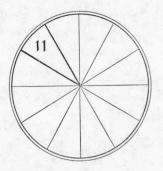

ELEVENTH HOUSE

Expression: Resultant-succedent/concentrative
Significators: Saturn and Uranus

KEYNOTE: The experiences of social expression and group integration and the identification of one's self with one's social function.

Traditional Meanings: Hopes, wishes, and goals. Friends and social life.

Abstract Meanings: How one externalizes his or her social function and how it influences his or her personal, inner life. Reform and revolutions. Group integration, new ideas, and individualistic orientations toward relationships.

Synastric Meanings: The experience of becoming thoroughly integrated into a group or collectivity of individuals. How two or more persons can best integrate their personal relationship with the needs and values of a larger group.

Types of Relationships: Associations with others on a professional and/or political level. Relationships that focus on developing new or unconventional forms of group activity.

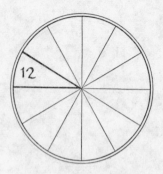

TWELFTH HOUSE

Expression: Resultant-cadent/dispersive
Significators: Jupiter and Neptune

KEYNOTE: The experience of realizing that what transpires at any one moment is a phase of an entire cyclic process linking the past with the future and potentiality with actuality.

Traditional Meanings: Karma, fate, obstacles, confinements, and unknown enemies.

Abstract Meanings: Accumulated resources. The resolution of conflicts between individual and society, the equalization of individual expression and collective needs. The unconscious, both personal and collective. The closing phase of any cycle of relationship that carries within it the most essential experiences of the past, from which a new cycle may grow.

Synastric Meanings: The underlying, unknown, or mysterious elements of a relationship, and its karmic implications.

Types of Relationships: Relationships that help the participants in realizing the unity underlying their life experiences. Relationships carried on in secret, mysterious, or isolated circumstances.

HOUSE-ORIENTED POSITIONS

If two individuals both have a planet exactly in the middle of the first house, the planets involved compose a house-oriented conjunction—even though they may be nowhere near one another, or even forming another aspect, from a zodiacal orientation. The house-oriented position of a planet is calculated by dividing the number of degrees a planet is from the cusp of a house by the total number of degrees in that particular house, then multiplying by thirty. This number is then converted to its position in the 360-degree cycle according to the sequence of the house the planet is in (see Chapter 9 for more details).

House-oriented positions are particularly significant for synastric use because they enable us to use the aspects existing between the natal planets of two persons from the perspective of the houses. Likewise, if two planets are situated exactly 120 degrees from one another from a house orientation, they would be regarded as composing a house-oriented trine, and so on. We will be using house-oriented positions and aspects extensively in Part Three.

7. THE SIGNS

A great deal of confusion is often generated by the fact that there are two totally independent zodiacs. Most astrologers use the zodiac of signs, produced by the apparent orbit of the sun around the Earth, called also "the ecliptic of the zodiac," and sometimes referred to as "the tropical zodiac." The zodiac of signs has four important turning points marked by the equinoxes and solstices. On the equinoxes (vernal and autumnal) the sun rises and sets directly to the east and west. On the first day of summer (the summer solstice) and the first day of winter (the winter solstice) the sun rises in its most extreme northeast and southeast positions, respectively. The twelve signs of the zodiac are derived by simply dividing this entire annual cycle by twelve, giving three signs of thirty degrees each to each season.

The other zodiac is the zodiac of constellations or the sidereal zodiac, composed of twelve star groups that bear the same names as the signs of the zodiac. There has been a good deal of controversy over which of these two zodiacs is the correct one for astrological use. During the early part of this century a small group of scientifically oriented astrologers reported that the sidereal zodiac was the one used by the ancient Egyptians. Concluding that the ancients must be correct (and not considering the fact that they also used the zodiac of signs) the sidereal astrologers claimed that for the past two thousand years astrologers had been using the wrong zodiac. According to the exponents of this school of thought, the two zodiacs coincided around the beginning of the Christian era, but the precession of the equinoxes (accounting for an increasing distance of one degree every seventy-two years between the two zodiacs) brings the difference today to almost thirty degrees. If one's sun sign is Scorpio in the tropical zodiac, a sidereal astrologer would call it Libra according to the constellations. The situation is further confused by conflicting theories about the exact beginnings/ endings of the constellations and the actual increment between the two zodiacs.

Deeper implications of the constellational zodiac and its relation with the 26,000-year Great Polar Cycle is a subject pursued in detail by Rudhyar in his book, *Astrological Timing*. Because the sidereal zodiac lacks an individual factor and therefore bears little relevance to most human beings, the zodiac used here is the zodiac of signs.

THE INTERNAL PATTERN OF THE ZODIAC OF SIGNS

The zodiac of signs is structured around the four cardinal points —the equinoxes and solstices. The equinoxes are the two days of the year when days and nights are equal in length. The solstices are the two days of the year when days and nights are most unequal—the summer solstice having the longest day of the year and the winter solstice having the longest night.

The span between the spring (vernal) equinox and the autumnal equinox is the time when the day forces—differentiation and per- sonalization—are dominant in the earth's organic cyclic process. From the autumnal equinox until the spring equinox the night forces —collectivization and universalization—are dominant.

The two hemispheres created by the axis of the equinoxes can be further divided into four quadrants by the solstitial axis. Here the span between the vernal equinox and the summer solstice can be seen as a period of intense organic growth, naturally following the birth of a new cycle. The sun is now rapidly moving northward and the nights grow longer.

At the moment of the summer solstice the sun reaches its maximum northern position, turns toward the south, and the nights naturally begin to grow shorter. Personalizing factors emerge as the rush for growth ebbs.

The autumnal equinox marks once more an equilibrium between days and nights. During the span between the autumnal equinox and the winter solstice, the socializing and in-gathering forces of nature are at the fore, as the nights once more become longer than the days.

Finally, the winter solstice brings the longest night. The night forces then begin to decline as the sun moves from the south to the equator. The future remains in the seed, able to give birth to a new cycle of manifestation at the vernal equinox.

The Cycle of the Elements.   Every sign is described by an *element* that refers to the type of substance it expresses. There are four elements, each connected with a triad of signs spaced 120 degrees apart in the zodiac.

The *fire* element represents the principle of vitality, animation, and action. It expresses itself through intense, emotional, individual channels. Fire is the element assigned to the sign of the vernal equinox, Aries, as well as to Leo and Sagittarius.

The *earth* element is associated with Capricorn, the sign of the winter solstice, along with the signs Virgo and Taurus. It refers to the practical, mundane, and collective affairs of life as well as to the principle of stability and security.

The *air* element represents the principle of adaptability and is connected with the intellect. It is assigned to Libra, the sign of the autumnal equinox, Gemini, and Aquarius.

The *water* element is associated with the sign of the summer solstice, Cancer, as well as with Scorpio and Pisces. It refers to energies of a sensory, emotional, and creative nature.

The Cycle of the Modes.   The signs are further described by modes, that express how the energies of the zodiac are released. The modes are derived by the threefold division of the zodiac, resulting in each of the three modes being assigned to four signs, spaced 90 degrees apart.

The *cardinal* or initiatory mode is the form of energy released at the equinoxes and solstices, thus associated with the signs Aries, Cancer, Libra, and Capricorn. It represents the principle of change and momentum. Cardinal signs generate power.

The *fixed* or focal mode is assigned to Taurus, Leo, Scorpio, and Aquarius. The fixed mode concentrates and focalizes the power released by the cardinal signs. The fixed signs represent the principle of structure and definition, giving depth and meaning to the cardinal experience. The fifteenth degree of each of the fixed signs is of particular importance, representing a point of maximum intensity midway between equinox and solstice where power is found in its most concentrated form.

The *mutable* or common mode distributes the power generated by the cardinal signs and focused by the fixed signs. It symbolizes the principle of flexibility and adaptability. The mutable mode is assigned to the signs Gemini, Virgo, Sagittarius, and Pisces.

THE MEANING OF THE SIGNS

The signs of the zodiac represent twelve basic types of human nature and energy utilization. The signs describe the way in which archetypal or collective human behavior and activity are manifested within an individual person or relationship. Brief meanings of the individual signs follow, with special attention to their synastric applications.

ARIES—the first sign.

Quality: Cardinal/fire
Significators: Mars and Pluto

KEYNOTE: The originating impulse, giving vitality and a sense of selfhood to an individualized consciousness just emerging from the sea of the unconscious. Impulse energy.

Traditional Meanings: Initiative, desire, courage, will, and impulsiveness.

Abstract Meanings: The central self and the essential structure of one's vital being. The equalization of the day and night forces leading to a new cycle of organic life.

Synastric Meanings: Energy directed toward initiating new relationships and one's use of initiative in general. How a contact affects one's sense of self. The essential quality of a relationship.

Types of Relationships: Impulsive relationships that assist individuals in their process of self-discovery.

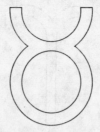

TAURUS—the second sign.

Quality: Fixed/earth
Significator: Venus

KEYNOTE: Energetic self-exertion as a means of establishing Arian impulses in a tangible form. Energy as substance.

Traditional Meanings: Inertia, determination, forcefulness, possessiveness, and practicality.

Abstract Meanings: Methodical orientations. The identification of self with substance. The focalization of Arian energies, giving them depth and meanings.

Synastric Meanings: The immediate resources and energies of a relationship. The substances one needs from an association. How two or more persons can co-operate together in a practical fashion.

Types of Relationships: Financial contacts or relationships that focus primarily on substance and materials.

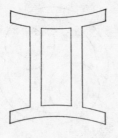

GEMINI—the third sign.

Quality: Mutable/air
Significator: Mercury

KEYNOTE: The channeling of energies toward association with the environment for the expansion of worldly knowledge. Mental energy.

Traditional Meanings: Changeability, duality, and restlessness. Academic and literary matters.

Abstract Meanings: The mind functioning on a subjective level. Associating, communicating, and recognizing the most obvious forms of relationship. The creation and development of systems and techniques.

Synastric Meanings: The mental, communicative energy involved in any relationship. How two or more persons can act together for the accumulation of knowledge and its practical application. What one can learn from a relationship.

Types of Relationships: Associations that emphasize the mental processes. Relationships that grow largely through letters and correspondence.

CANCER—the fourth sign.

Quality: Cardinal/water
Significator: The moon

KEYNOTE: The establishment of a central base for the future outward projection of personal energies. Centralized energy.

Traditional Meanings: Receptivity, the feelings and instincts. The home and family.

Abstract Meanings: Concrete selfhood and the establishment of a secure foundation for the expression of selfhood. The apex of organic growth. The longest day meets the shortest night (at the summer solstice) marking the beginning of the personalizing phase of the organic cycle.

Synastric Meanings: The basic foundation of a relationship and one's capacity for sharing a central source of energy with others. Emotional receptivity and the expression of feelings. What one needs emotionally from a relationship.

Types of Relationships: Family contacts and cohabitation. Emotionally secure relationships.

LEO—the fifth sign.

Quality: Fixed/fire
Significator: The sun

KEYNOTE: *The urge to dynamically and creatively express one's self through all that one does. Self-expressive energy.*

Traditional Meanings: Self-confidence, self-expression, creativity, flamboyance, pleasure, and the emotions.

Abstract Meanings: The drive toward dramatically externalizing one's self for the purpose of self-satisfaction and social recognition. The individual, once secure in his identity (Cancer), seeks to broaden his sphere of activity by displaying to others who he is and what he can do.

Synastric Meanings: Expressing one's inner, creative self through spontaneous interplay with others. How an association can further one's self-confidence and creative expression. What an individual needs to express through relationship.

Types of Relationships: Contacts that inspire confidence and creativity. Romantic relationships.

VIRGO—the sixth sign.

Quality: Mutable/earth
Significator: Mercury

KEYNOTE: *The reorientation of one's emotional energies as a preparation for objective participation in the outer world. Repolarization of energy.*

Traditional Meanings: Fastidiousness, discrimination, introspection, detail, study, health, service, and employment.

Abstract Meanings: Discrimination and critical analysis. Personal reorientation, self-criticism, and the process of self-perfection. The control and regulation of self-expression.

Synastric Meanings: A relationship's capacity to resolve inner conflicts. The analysis of the dynamics behind a relationship. Discrimination toward others and toward contacts with others.

Types of Relationships: Therapeutic and employer-employee relationships.

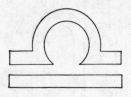

LIBRA—the seventh sign.

Quality: Cardinal/air

Significator: Venus

KEYNOTE: Energy utilized for the purpose of bringing individuals together and harmonizing their relationships. The energy of attraction-repulsion.

Traditional Meanings: Idealism, beauty, and balance. Social consciousness and relationships in general.

Abstact Meanings: Consciousness functioning in the objective mode through co-operating and associating with others. The equalization of the day and night forces (autumnal equinox) leading to social interactivity.

Synastric Meanings: The energy that brings individuals together or drives them apart. The basic potentialities of a relationship. The type of energy an individual can give to an association and what he or she expects from relationships in general.

Types of Relationships: Marriage and relationships of a serious nature with agreed-upon terms and responsibilities.

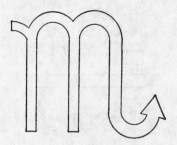

SCORPIO—the eighth sign.

Quality: Fixed/water
Significators: Mars and Pluto

KEYNOTE: Sex energy or the power inherent whenever individuals come together as equals and exchange vital energies.

Traditional Meanings: Sex, jealousy, death, will power, magic, and occultism. The regeneration of personal energies.

Abstract Meanings: The drive to become one with others in order to participate together as a greater whole. The process of individuation. Creative tension.

Synastric Meanings: The urge to merge with another and the driving force behind interpersonal relationships. The transformative aspect of a relationship. What an individual needs on a sexual/spiritual level.

Types of Relationships: Equalized, person-to-person interchanges that penetrate to the center of self. Tantric sex.

SAGITTARIUS—the ninth sign.

Quality: Mutable/fire
Significator: Jupiter

KEYNOTE: *Energy directed toward the abstract mind for the purpose of understanding the universal significance of creative relationships as they manifest in all spheres of meaning. Synthesizing energy.*

Traditional Meanings: Religion, philosophy, inspiration. Sports, higher education, and law.

Abstract Meanings: The abstract, archetypal mind. Social/cultural matters. Recognizing and correlating relationships within relationships.

Synastric Meanings: The expansive qualities of a relationship. How a relationship can enrich one's understanding and personal philosophy. The social, cultural values behind an association and the ideals one needs to have confirmed by his companions.

Types of Relationships: Associations that encourage the participants to expand their social, cultural, philosophical horizons.

CAPRICORN—the tenth sign.

Quality: Cardinal/earth
Significator: Saturn

KEYNOTE: Energies utilized for the purpose of expanding and securing one's place in the outer world. Collective energy.

Traditional Meanings: Social conventions, status, ambition, and politics. The state and political power.

Abstract Meanings: Social integration and collective functions. The person as a social entity. The longest night meets the shortest day (the winter solstice) as the in-gathering forces are at their apex.

Synastric Meanings: How a particular relationship fits into the larger social/collective context. An association's significance in terms of one's social position and security. An individual's responsibility to a relationship.

Types of Relationships: One's relationship to his or her culture and nation and, in a larger sense, to the cosmos.

AQUARIUS—the eleventh sign.

Quality: Fixed/air
Significators: Uranus and Saturn

KEYNOTE: The channeling of energy toward the social expression of new values, ideals, and life styles. Socially expressed energy.

Traditional Meanings: Political movements and revolutions. Science, music, and humanitarianism. Group values.

Abstract Meanings: Social expression and the externalization of one's social function. The capacity to create and express one's self in broad cultural terms.

Synastric Meanings: The balance of individual expression with collective need or will. How one can express one's self through group situations. What an individual needs to give to a relationship or to a larger whole.

Types of Relationships: Group or mass contact with others. Unconventional relationships. The concept of universal brotherhood. Societies and associations.

PISCES—the twelfth sign.

Quality: Mutable/water
Significators: Neptune and Jupiter

KEYNOTE: Psychic energy or energy that is receptive toward the essential universality of life.

Traditional Meanings: Mysticism, fanaticism, devotion, impressionability, and openness. Drugs and ESP.

Abstract Meanings: Psychic sensitivity and threshold experiences. The need to repolarize from collective to individual values. Compassion and the intuitive recognition of universal oneness.

Synastric Meanings: The psychic and universalizing elements of a relationship. A relationship's link with the past and its more mysterious or unknown aspects.

Types of Relationships: Associations that enable the individuals in understanding the universality of life. Relationships that focus on the use of psychic energies.

THE SABIAN SYMBOLS

In 1925 Marc Edmund Jones recorded, with the assistance of a clairvoyant, a remarkable series of poetic images that symbolically describes the 360 degrees of the zodiac (or any cycle of unfoldment). Dane Rudhyar, who was largely responsible for introducing the Sabian symbols (as Marc Jones named them) to the general astrological public, worked extensively with them for the following half century. In his treatise on the Sabian symbols, *An Astrological Mandala: The Cycle of Transformations and its 360 Symbolical Phases*, which includes the entire series of 360 symbols, Rudhyar writes:

> What makes this whole production [of the Sabian symbols] almost incredible is that while it operated purely at random and at a fantastic speed, the result was a series of symbols which, when carefully studied, are shown to possess a definite and very complex internal structure. [p. 26]

The Sabian symbols are guides to the more delicate and subtle interpretation of any astrological factor (planets, angles, planetary midpoints and parts, etc.) in terms of their zodiacal positions and especially from the house and phase orientations. For instance, the degree symbol for thirteen Scorpio (phase 223)—*an inventor performing a laboratory experiment*—reflects the stage of cyclic development that occurs at the two hundred and twenty-third segment of any cycle of 360 degrees, be it the thirteenth zodiacal degree of Scorpio, a point in the sky corresponding to the thirteenth segment of the eighth house, or a phase arc of 223 degrees. The symbols, as Rudhyar explains,

> do not deal exclusively with the degrees of the zodiac. They refer to the division of any cyclic life process into 360 degrees; for this reason I have stressed *the phase number* of the symbol as much as the zodiacal degree to which it refers. The essential

point to remember is that we are dealing with a life process; we might say a cosmic process, but in any case it is a gradual process of actualization of a set of new potentialities. [*An Astrological Mandala*, p. 30]

The Sabian symbols can be used extensively through investigations of birth and synastric charts to reach a deeper comprehension of the more subtle and underlying implications of selfhood and relatedness.

8. PLANETARY COMBINATIONS

In the preceding chapters of this part we explained that planetary motions and cycles (which can be viewed against the background of several possible frames of reference: the aspects, houses, signs, etc.) are at the foundation of any approach to astrology, and that since no two planets have identical orbits, every planet is engaged in a constantly changing angular relationship with every other planet —producing the phases and aspects. Here we shall describe the meaning and function of some of the most significant planetary pairs, from a synastric view, and have a look at their cyclic mid-points and planetary parts.

In astrology the planets symbolize the ten essential human functions. In addition to the ten primary functions, there are forty-five secondary functions (departments of life symbolized by forty-five possible dyadic combinations of the ten planets: sun-moon; sun-Mercury; sun-Venus, etc.). When comparing the planets in two people's charts the pairs are increased to fifty-five because one's sun can be paired with the other's sun, one's moon with the other's moon, and so on. One can also pair the angles and the lunar nodes with the planets, as well as investigate triadic combinations.

The role and meaning of any planetary pair (or triad) is derived by synthesizing the functions of the factors involved. The relationship existing between the planetary pair of Mars and Venus, for instance, symbolizes, in a natal chart, the personal function and implications of human relatedness—how one's emotional, creative, and sexual natures are structured, the actional principle of Mars combined with the receptive-evaluative principle of Venus. The phase arc, the houses, and the signs occupied by Mars and Venus in the birth chart will reveal the quality (phase arc or aspect) of the planetary relationship and the experiences (houses) and energies (signs) through which one can best fulfill his or her relationships with others in the personal, individual sphere. The dyad of Mars and Venus in synastric charts describes creative and sexual potentialities of the interpersonal relationship.

MUTUAL PAIRS

The mutual pairs are those in which a particular planet (or other factor) of one birth chart is compared with the same planet of another chart. Brief interpretations of each mutual pair (including the angles and the lunar nodes) follow.

Sun to Sun: How the individuals' life purposes and temperaments integrate with one another. The manner in which the two can best relate directly, particularly on a long-term basis. The *vital* function of a relationship.

Moon to Moon: The characteristic way that the individuals can best live together in a day-to-day fashion. The blending of their emotional temperaments and senses of receptivity. The *receptive, mediating* principle of relationship.

Mercury to Mercury: The approach from which two individuals can best connect with one another through the medium of verbal communication. The potentiality of the relationship as a mind-to-mind association. The *communicative, associative* function of relationship.

Venus to Venus: How the individuals can best blend their receptive senses of inner value and appreciation. The manner in which they can best interact in terms of realizing inner truths. The *appreciative, internalizing* aspect of relationship.

Mars to Mars: The way in which two individuals might most successfully combine their personal energies of expression for the achievement of a common goal. The potentiality of the association for the release of energy. The *expressive, externalizing* function of the relationship.

Jupiter to Jupiter: A combination of two individuals' drives toward social expansion. The relationship's potential on the level of social participation and acceptance. The *expansive, participative* function of relationship.

Saturn to Saturn: The basic structure and limitations of a relationship. The way that the participants can best interact within a specific, defined field of activity. The *definitive, clarifying* function of relationship.

Uranus to Uranus: The individuals' abilities to assist one another in going beyond social conventions. The transformative potentialities of a relationship. The way that the individuals can best share unusual, unconventional, or unexpected experiences. The *transformative* function of relationship.

Neptune to Neptune: How two individuals can best combine forces on the psychic and transcendental levels for the realization of universal oneness. The *universalizing* function of relationship.

Pluto to Pluto: The regenerative potentialities of a relationship. How the individuals can renew themselves by emerging into a new realm of consciousness. The *reformulative* function of relationship.

Ascendant to Ascendant: The contact between two persons on the level of individuality. The best synthesis of their unique and special qualities for the pursuit of a mutual reality. The *individualizing* aspect of relationship.

M.C. to M.C.: How two individuals can assist each other in realizing their respective places and functions in the social and spiritual community. The *social, political, and spiritual* aspects of relationship.

Lunar Node to Lunar Node: The lunar nodes represent, natally, one's individual line of karma (the south lunar node) and dharma (the north lunar node). In synastry the relationship between nodes is quite significant because they indicate, in addition to the karmic implications of an association, mutual emotional and psychic sensitivity.

The synastric conjunction/opposition aspect between nodes is particularly interesting. The entire nodal cycle requires 18.6 years to complete, so that if two individuals are 9.3 years of age apart, one's north node would be conjunct the other's south node and vice versa, indicating mutual emotional and psychic sensitivity, and a relationship that links the past of one person with the future unfoldment of the other. In instances where the two north nodes are conjunct (implying a conjunction between the south nodes as well), the two individuals share similar karmic-dharmic paths.

The significance of mutual pairs (as archetypally described above) in a specific interpersonal relationship can be determined by the disposition of the particular planets (or other factors) in the natal charts (in terms of house, zodiacal longitude, and planetary relationships in the chart as a whole) as well as the place of the pair in the various synastric charts described in the following chapter. The zodiacal positions symbolize the energies brought together within the department of life symbolized by the combination. The houses involved reveal qualities of individual experience that may be encountered through the facet of the relationship symbolized by the planets. The aspect or phase existing between the planets is representative of the essential quality of the interfunctional relationship symbolized by the planetary combination. Generally, an aspect based on duality (an opposition, square, or octile) represents a contact that is stimulating and exciting with some contrast between the individuals' functions that might manifest as frustrations and conflict or, if the underlying unity and complementary natures are understood, as a most constructive interaction. On the other hand, aspects based on three (the trine and the sextile) symbolize a harmonious, flowing association that, while smoother and possibly more productive (particularly the sextile) than any of the duality series of aspects, may be lacking their more definite, focused type of awareness. A quincunx aspect between planets indicates a contact that combines conflict with harmony. The quintile symbolizes a creative interchange and the septile a destiny-directed association.

To give an example, if one person's sun is in the fifth house, Gemini, and another's sun is in the ninth house, Scorpio, the two individuals may encounter a combined experience dealing with creative self-expression (fifth house) and the expansion of philosophical horizons (ninth house). The basic energies that will be tapped by the individuals in their pursuit of these experiences will combine the communicative mental energies of Gemini with Scorpio's penetrating, sexual energies. If the two suns' house-oriented positions are close to 120 degrees apart (the fifth house to the ninth house), one's way of experiencing creative self-expression (fifth house) should inspire and flow well with the other's way of experiencing the expansion of his or her understanding of the scheme of the universe (ninth house). If the phase arc between the two suns' zodiacal longitudes (Gemini to Scorpio) is near to 150 degrees (quincunx) or 155 degrees (tri-septile), however, the solar facet of the association should be strongly stimulated and open to conflict, change, and the unexpected in the way the two individuals blend their vital energies. Because of these distinctions (between the house-oriented and zodiacal phase arcs) it could be said that while the exchange of vital energies between the individuals may be open to a great many variations (zodiacal phase arc), the experiences that are brought about through the exchange of such energies are most likely to be of a harmonious nature (house-oriented trine).

INTERFUNCTIONAL COMBINATIONS

In addition to the matching of the same planets in two people's charts as discussed above, there are dozens of possible combinations linking two or three unlike factors. What follows is an attempt to present the most basic of these combinations from a synastric perspective.

The Symbols of Self. The most essential factors of any astrological chart, from either a natal or synastric approach, are the axes of the horizon and the meridian (the angles) and the two "lights" (the sun and the moon). They represent the inner centers of personality; they are the astrological symbols of self. The contacts between these factors are most significant and symbolize the foundations of interpersonal relationship.

Relationship is multifaceted; a single interpersonal contact has implications on every level of existence and reflects within itself the entire universe of which it is a part. When two or more individuals come together in a relationship, anything can happen. Astrology can help us in understanding the essential focus of the association and what might happen, not so much in terms of events alone as in the personal crises and transformations that underlie the events, in fulfillment of the inner potential of the relationship. The synastric contacts between the sun, moon, and angles symbolize deep aspects of a relationship, aspects that may transcend the personality level of human consciousness. They reveal the central characteristics and potentials of the liaison as well as the channels through which all other peripheral experiences are assimilated. Perhaps the most revealing indicators of a relationship's significance for one's self are the phase arcs, both zodiacal and house-oriented, between one's sun, moon, and angles and another's. A very close aspect (within an orb of about one degree) between at least one of the sixteen combinations of the sun, moon, and angles indicates that there is a very intimate contact existing between the two individuals, a channel of contact that can potentially accommodate almost any type of peripheral relationship. If there is not a strong contact linking one of the pair, or if the channel is obstructed, the peripheral interpersonal functions (each remaining planetary pair symbolizing one such function) such as mental association, sexual activity, and so on probably will not make much of a contribution in terms of the development of the individuals' consciousness beyond the realm of personality—of mundane acting, feeling, and thinking. If there is a strong link between persons on the level of self and individuality—symbolized by the sun, moon, and angles—then whatever contact transpires between the participants within the realm of personality is more likely to consciously serve as a growth experience and a channel of individual expression.

Sun to Moon: The soli-lunar relationship is the most fundamental of all astrological cycles composed of two celestial bodies and is often considered to be the archetypal cycle of relationship. It is archetypal because it deals with the processes most basic in the development of life on Earth. It is clearly visible in the constantly changing appearance of the moon: The moon's relationship with the sun, seen from the perspective of the Earth, is what is actually changing, the moon reflecting the constantly changing relationship.

It is believed by many occultists that life on Earth has not yet evolved to the point where organisms can directly assimilate the light forces of the sun. The lunar principle is needed to mediate the solar light force for Earth, transforming it into organic life forms. In *The Lunation Cycle*, Rudhyar writes that the moon

> is the mediatrix, mother or Muse, whose function is to cater to the needs of the evolving units constituting collectively the substance of the cycle. She distributes solar potential (i.e., spiritual food and energy) through organic and psychological agencies which she builds to fit the need of evolving material units, be they cells or personalities. She therefore is the servant of both earth and sun. She releases the *light* of the sun and by so doing serves the needs of earth creatures for organic and psychic *life*. [p. 24–25]

In the comparison of two natal charts, the sun-moon dyad indicates how the sun person's temperament and life purpose can be nourished by the moon person's receptivity, and how the moon person's feelings and instincts can be guided by the sun person's sense of meaning.

Sun to Angles: Indicates how the sun person's vitality and sense of purpose can be integrated with the angle person's sense of individual selfhood.

Moon to Angles: Symbolizes how one's most unique and individual qualities of selfhood can combine with another's receptivity to the needs of self and others.

A conjunction aspect between the sun, moon, or angles denotes that the individuals should be able to identify with one another in the functions symbolized by whatever factors are conjunct. A synastric opposition, square, or octile aspect between the sun, moon, or angles is representative of a relationship that could result in a very constructive type of creative tension (if contrasting temperaments can be consolidated and not dominated by conflict and separatism) in which the participants are keenly stimulated by one another's sense of self. A trine or sextile link between factors symbolizes a harmonious understanding of one another's individuality and life purposes.

The Symbols of Association and Participation. The planets Jupiter and Mercury are connected with the activities of association and participation with others. Mercury is the archetype of all forms of mental communication; Jupiter signifies the individual as a social entity openly participating with others for the attainment of a social ideal. Jupiter is also symbolic of the preservation and increase of the established order of things and the instruction of individuals concerning "the rules of the game" they will have to follow in order to succeed. In this way the dyad of Jupiter-Mercury has been related to the educative process.

In synastry the Jupiter-Mercury pair can be representative of a relationship's potentiality for mutual social participation and the exchange of ideas. That is, it indicates how the individuals can best learn from one another and assist one another in realizing their social, cultural ideals.

The Symbols of Expression and Appreciation. Mars and Venus relate to the process of personalization. Two opposite modes of personal functions are synthesized in their pairing—the internalization, appreciation, and judgment signified by Venus, and the action and externalization of energies following judgment represented by Mars. Natally, the Mars-Venus dyad polarizes one's emotional, creative, and sexual natures and represents one's most intimate realization of the fundamental duality underlying life. A close look at the relationship between these two planets in a particular chart can reveal the best way for a person to fulfill his or her destiny through personal relationships with others.

The Mars pole of this axis represents archetypal masculine or actional energy, standing for the basic urge—in everyone, regardless of sex—to externalize, to go forth into the world and make an impression on it. On the other pole is Venus, archetypal feminine or receptive energy, the urge to reach a state of communion with one's self and others, as well as the capacity for internalization of experience and for the appreciation of the relationship. As a polarized unit, Mars-Venus describes the masculine/feminine psychological components as an interplay of interdependent, inseparable opposites.

In a birth chart the phase of Mars-Venus, and the house and sign positions of Mars and Venus, symbolizes how one best use relationships with others as a means of self-actualization.

In a synastric chart the disposition of Mars and Venus is symbolic of the creative, emotional, and sexual potentials of a relationship. A square, opposition, or octile aspect between one's Mars and another's Venus denotes an intense, passionate contact that could make for an exciting love affair as well as an inspiring creative relationship. A trine or sextile aspect between this combination signifies a comfortable emotional contact that offers security and endurance.

The Symbols of Individual/Collective Interpenetration. The planets Jupiter and Saturn combined have to do with the interplay between an individual and the society or culture of which he or she is a part or, on a larger scale, between humanity as a whole and the planet Earth, of which humanity is a part, with a definite function to fulfill in the destiny of the planet. Saturn is the archetypal structural principle, symbolic of ego and identity. The Saturnian function gives definite form and focus to all things, out of which arises individualized consciousness. Jupiter, the opposite pole of this dyad, represents the individual as a social entity and the society within which he operates. The phase arc of Jupiter-Saturn, along with the houses and signs of the two planets in the natal chart, indicates ways in which an individual can best fulfill his or her destiny as a unique and responsive member of a greater whole.

In a synastric chart, the Jupiter-Saturn pair represents how two people can best co-operate for the purpose of giving social-cultural relevancy to their individual existences.

CYCLIC MIDPOINTS

There are two factors that can be used as further indices describing the relationship between two planets: the *midpoints* and *parts*.

A planetary midpoint is the point in space exactly midway between two planetary bodies. Midpoints were actually developed several centuries ago. The first astrologer known to use them (though others may have preceded him) was Guido Bonati, born in 1230, the court astrologer of Emperor Fredrick II. Bonati used midpoints largely as a means of rectifying uncertain birth times: it was his belief that all people were born at times when either a planet was on one of the four angles of the chart or when a midpoint between two planets was so positioned.

Midpoints gradually faded out of practice after Bonati's death, but were revived by the Hamburg astrologer Albert Knieph during the latter part of the nineteenth century. He introduced midpoints to Alfred Witte, the founder of the Uranian system of astrology, who in turn introduced them to Reinhold Ebertin. Through Ebertin's book *The Combination of Stellar Influences* (Aalen, Germany: Ebertin-Verlag: 1940, 1972), natal planetary midpoints have become widely known and are being used by astrologers all over the world.

What has been completely overlooked concerning planetary midpoints, however, is that they are expressions of a cyclic phase relationship. The conventional way of calculating midpoints (or halfsums) is to divide the *nearest* arc of zodiacal space between two bodies by two. There is an important shortcoming in this method: By simply taking the nearest arc between two planets, one does not take into consideration whether the cycle of relationship between the two bodies is in its *waxing phase* or in its *waning phase*. That is, a relationship between two planets moving from the conjunction (o degree arc) to the opposition (180 degree arc) and a relationship that has already reached the opposition and is progressing toward the next conjunction have different meanings, just as the first-quarter moon differs in meaning from the third-quarter moon.

When the cycle of relationship existing between two planets is in its waxing phase—when the faster moving planet is progressing along a path that will lead to an opposition aspect before the next conjunction is reached—the purpose of the relationship is directed toward the development of potentials, the building of organic structures, and the processes of involution and specialization. Here feelings and instinctual actions are dominant, since abstract consciousness is in the process of permeating physical organisms. During the waning phase—when the faster of the two planets is moving away from opposition and toward conjunction—the purpose of the relationship is to release and expand the consciousness that has been contained within the structures and organisms built up during the waxing hemicycle. In this phase mental activities and evolutionary forces are dominant.

Spatial midpoints, as we have seen, are determined by bisecting the nearest arc between two planets. They are the conventional midpoints, or half-sums, calculated by dividing in half the sum of the zodiacal longitudes of two planets. *Cyclic midpoints* are the result of dividing in half the space between two bodies in the direction in which their cycle is developing. Of course, in the case of a waxing phase relationship (before opposition has occurred), the spatial and cyclic midpoints are the same; and when two planets are in their waning phase the cyclic midpoint is always exactly 180 degrees ahead of the spatial midpoint in zodiacal space. Figures 12 and 13 are meant to clarify these distinctions.

Natal cyclic midpoints can be easily calculated by dividing the planetary pair's phase arc by two and adding the result to the position of the slower-moving body.

For example: Mars 17°46′ Taurus and Venus 20°26′ Virgo

$$122°40′ \quad \text{(phase arc)} \div 2 = 61°20′$$
$$61°20′ \quad \text{Half of phase arc}$$
$$+ \ 47°46′ \quad (17°46′ \text{ Taurus) slower planet}$$
$$\overline{109°06′} \quad (19°06′ \text{ Cancer) cyclic midpoint}$$

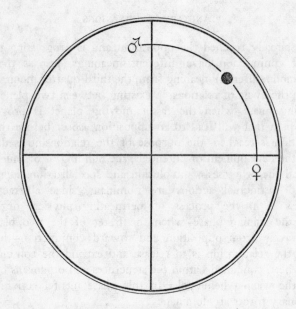

Figure 12

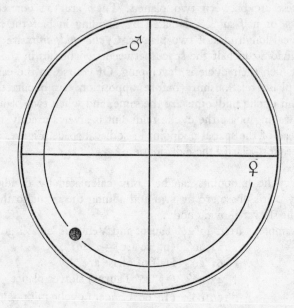

Figure 13

In calculating synastric midpoints the synastric phase arc is divided by two and added to the older person's natal planet of the synastric pair.

For example: Sun 10°30′ Gemini (older person) and
moon 10°30′ Leo (younger person)

    60°00′ (phase arc) ÷ 2 = 30°00′

    30°00′ half of phase arc

 + 70°30′ (10°30′ Gemini) older person's

   100°30′ (10°30′ Cancer) cyclic midpoint

HOW TO USE PLANETARY MIDPOINTS

The primary structure of any planetary relationship is the cycle, and any deep analysis of planetary relationships logically begins and ends with a consideration of the particular cyclic phase existing between a pair of planets. Aspects, "Arabian Parts," and midpoints are all functions of a cycle of relationship. They are *expressions* of the particular phase of the cycle. The cycle is a function, in turn, of the evolution and actualization of the archetypal relationship symbolized by the two planets involved. Every cycle of relationship, as we have seen, is made up of waxing and waning hemicycles. Every cycle passes from conjunction to opposition to conjunction again. The length of time required to complete an entire cycle is determined by the orbits of the planets. The purpose to be fulfilled through the experiences connected with the unfoldment of this cyclic relationship is revealed in the synthesis of these two planets and the house and zodiacal degree of their most recent conjunction.

Because midpoints are functions of phase relationships, in the interpretation of an astrological chart they are best used as a step following the consideration of the phase arc existing between two planets. The phase gives us an overview of the purpose and meaning of a planetary cycle as it is operating in terms of the individual's personality or in terms of an interpersonal relationship. The midpoints derived from the phase arc then give a specific and detailed view of the cyclic relationship. For instance, while the cycle of Mars and Venus and its position in one's birth chart symbolizes how one can best use relationships with others in a harmonious fashion along the path of actualization, the midpoints of these two planets signifies the area of experience (house) and type of energy (sign) most available to the individual for the purpose of bringing out and fulfilling in a functional manner his or her potentialities for relationship. In comparing two charts, the midpoint between one's Mars and another's Venus reveals the focus of the relationship in the creative, emotional, sexual sphere.

Direct and Indirect Midpoints. From a thoroughly cyclic approach we are not so much interested in a singular midpoint but in a midpoint *axis* composed of two opposed midpoints: a "direct" midpoint and an "indirect" midpoint. Both ends of such an axis are significant, representing distinct yet inseparable functions of cyclic relationship.

While the direct midpoint always occupies a point in zodiacal space enclosed within the phase arc of the two planets, the indirect midpoint always occupies a point in space that is outside the boundaries of the phase arc. Upon this foundation we can interpret the distinctions between the meanings of the two polar opposites of the midpoint axis.

These two ends of the midpoint axis can be seen as representing the dichotomies past-future, external-internal, and actual-potential. The direct midpoint represents the experience and circumstances (house position) and the activity and energy (zodiacal position) within which the purpose and quality of the relationship (determined by the nature of the two planets, their phase arc, and their house and sign positions) is most focused and operable in an external manner. It symbolizes what potentialities represented by the last conjunction of the two bodies have already been actualized in the past: the ancestral past, reincarnations, one's karma, etc. It is representative of what the personality has most likely already developed through the synthesis of the two planets composing the cycle. That is, the direct midpoint is a symbol for the manner in which the archetypal potentialities of the synthesis (conjunction) of the two planetary functions may be best, and most readily, expressed in an external manner.

The indirect midpoint, then, relates to the future—to the area of experience and the type of activity yet to be integrated into the fabric of the bi-polar planetary relationship—to potentialities most ripe for actualization. Indirect midpoints often relate to the most focused and intense point of the *internalization* and *personalization* of the planetary relationship as well. Direct midpoints indicate the general focus and balance of what should have already been integrated into the individuality and/or interpersonal relationship from past experiences and relationships. They are points of actual fulfillment and capabilities. Indirect midpoints indicate the focus and pivot for that which one should strive to actualize—capabilities and experiences yet to be acquired.

Summing Up. Midpoints reveal areas of intensity and strength in terms of external manifestation (direct midpoints) and inner potential (indirect midpoints). The specific meaning of any midpoint axis can be derived through the consideration of the functions of the two planets involved, their phase arc (and/or aspect), as well as the sign and house positions of the two bodies and the midpoints themselves. A significant yet often overlooked method for deriving the meaning of the midpoints is through the use of the Sabian symbols described in Chapter 7.

When a third planet is situated on a midpoint, the function of that planet should assist in the process of bringing the phase of the cyclic relationship symbolized by the pairing of the two planets whose midpoint is so related into clearer focus. When two separate pairs of planets share a common midpoint axis their respective relationships should be focused or manifested through a common facet.

Midpoints can give a new dimension to the meaning of an astrological chart—yet it is obvious from the vast number of possible midpoints that selectivity is necessary. An excessive concentration on midpoints—or any other astrological factor—might distract one's attention from other equally significant chart factors. How does one go about achieving a relevant selection of midpoints? It depends largely on the demands of the situation and the personal experience and preference of the astrologer. In many cases an adequate astrological interpretation can be accomplished without the consideration of midpoints at all. When a strenuous analysis of the less-apparent implications of a chart is called for, midpoints can be used to give a more thorough understanding of important developments within certain departments of life that are encountered along the path of unfoldment.

PLANETARY PARTS

Some of the Arabian astrologers of the first millennium A.D. were apparently inclined to pursue the more abstract and mathematical relationships inherent in an astrological chart. Among their devices are the mathematical or synthetic points, used as indices to the phase relationship between any two planets of a chart *in relation to* a third factor of the same chart, usually an angle or a house cusp.

As time went on, somewhat dubious names were assigned to many of these parts, names that supposedly described their "influences," (e.g., the Point of Fatality, the Point of Male Children, the Point of Private Enemies, the Point of Honorable and Illustrious Acquaintances, etc.). Most of what is today known about these "Arabian Parts" was recorded in *The Doctrine of Nativities* by John Gadsbury in the middle of the seventeenth century. Gadsbury, however, gives little insight into their philosophical or psychological meanings and applications, though it may have been he who assigned the above mentioned names.

Most modern astrological textbooks and most modern astrologers tend to use only the part of fortune, derived through a synthesis of the soli-lunar phase arc with the ascendant. A more expansive view of the implications inherent in selfhood and relationship can be approached by a study of all the planetary parts. In *The Astrology of Personality* Rudhyar describes planetary parts as

a kind of "group algebra" working out nearly endless correlations and permutations between original elements of the birth-formula. Its complexity makes it, of course, most unwieldy; yet there is no doubt that it represents the ultimate and most abstract type of astrological thought—that by means of which we come most closely to life itself and its multifarious network of relationships. [p. 306]

Parts are particularly significant from a phase orientation because they integrate planetary phases with the cross of the horizon-meridian (and the houses derived from that cross), the astrological framework most symbolic of the uniqueness of a person and his or her orientation to life. The planetary parts are highly individualized indicators of the ways in which a bi-planetary relationship can best be expressed.

While midpoints both signify focal centers through which the power generated by a planetary pair can be released in a dynamic form, and indicate experiences and energies that need to be integrated if the purpose of the cycle is to be fulfilled, parts reveal how a dyad can be expressed with the greatest ease in terms of the four angles. A natal part composed of a synthesis of a phase arc with the ascendant reveals how the particular planetary pair can best assist the person in coming to a better understanding of his or her unique individuality. When a phase arc is applied to the descendant, it produces a part that symbolizes how the person might best use the function of the planetary pair to deal with others and establish fruitful relationships. The areas of experience and the energies through which a person can use a planetary pair for the purpose of personal integration are shown by a part composed of a synthesis of a phase arc with the I.C.; in a complementary fashion, the part produced by the application of a phase arc to the M.C. expresses the path that should lead the individual to a fulfillment of his or her place and purpose socially and/or spiritually.

The parts are the most varied and diversified of all astrological factors. If we count only those parts derived from the cycles of relationship of the forty-five possible natal pairs of planets and their application to the twelve house cusps, we arrive at a total of 1,080 such parts. Even if we narrow it down to only those parts involving the four angles of the chart, we still have 360 distinct points of significance. Each planetary pair produces eight parts through the synthesis of its phase arc with each of the four angles when the phase arc is added as well as subtracted from the angles (see Figure 14). The parts produced by the addition of the phase arcs to the four points of the horizon-meridian are called *direct* parts; those produced by subtraction are called *retrograde* parts.

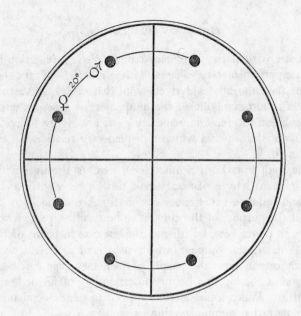

Figure 14

The *house* a part falls into is most important because it defines the experiences and circumstances through which the expression of the part is most likely to develop. For instance, when a part occupies the fifth house, the synthesis of the functions signified by the two planets and the angle is most likely to develop through experiences related to self-expression, children, creativity, etc.

Direct parts indicate the experiences and activities through which one can best achieve an unfoldment of the potential symbolized by the planetary relationship under consideration. This potential is revealed by the nature of the two planets, their houses, signs, and phase arc. The function of the faster-moving planet is emphasized in the direct part. It is calculated in the following manner:

Jupiter 27°41′ Libra, Saturn 19°7′ Cancer,
Ascendant 10°50′ Scorpio

220°50′	Ascendant (10°50′ Scorpio)
+ 98°34′	Phase Arc
319°24′	Direct Part (19°24′ Aquarius)

Retrograde parts internalize the quality of the bi-planetary relationship and give to it a deeply personal significance that might, like the indirect midpoint, be rooted in the past. Here the slower-moving planet can be seen as dominant and serving as a focus for inward turning energies. Retrograde parts are calculated in the following manner:

220°50'	Ascendant (10°50' Scorpio)
− 98°34'	Phase Arc
122°16'	Retrograde Part (2°16' Leo)

Through the use of planetary phase arcs, midpoints, and parts, an astrologer can come to a deeper understanding of how the function symbolized by any planetary pair should operate in terms of personality and individuality. While in most instances it is impractical to work with all the phase arcs, midpoints, and parts of an astrological chart, these abstract points can be of great value when there is need to pursue the deeper implications of a psychological or spiritual process signified by a planetary pair.

The natal parts of Mars-Venus as well as Jupiter and Saturn are particularly useful in synastry because they deal with sensitive areas of one's manner of participating in relationship.

THE PART OF VENUS-MARS AND THE ASCENDANT

Formula: Ascendant+Venus-Mars phase arc

The ascendant represents selfhood. A synthesis of Mars and Venus with the ascendant produces a part that is most intimately connected with one's potential in terms of experiences and expressions of emotionality through relationship. Its position in terms of natal house and sign symbolizes how one can become more in tune with his or her own unique creative, emotional, and sexual potentialities and his or her sensitivity to his or her self.

THE PART OF VENUS-MARS AND THE DESCENDANT

Formula: Descendant+Venus-Mars phase arc

The descendant symbolizes relationship. This part is directly opposite the above part and points to the area of life where one's potential for personal and intimate relationships may be most readily actualized. The house and sign of the birth chart occupied by this part symbolize the energy and experience through which the individual can most consciously and sensitively participate in meaningful relationships with others on an essentially personal level.

The dyad of Mars-Venus represents relationships of an essentially personal nature, operating on a *horizontal* plane; the pairing of Jupiter and Saturn is symbolical of *vertical* relationships, such as the interplay existing between an individual and society. Within this context Saturn—the archetypal structural force—represents ego identity. Saturn is the principle that gives definite form and focus to all things, out of which arises individualized consciousness. Jupiter, the opposite pole of this dyad, represents the individual as a social entity and the society within which he or she must operate. The positions and parts of Jupiter-Saturn in a birth chart serve as indicators for the ways in which one can best fulfill his or her destiny as a unique and responsive member of a greater whole.

THE PART OF JUPITER-SATURN AND THE I.C.

Formula: I.C.+Jupiter-Saturn phase arc

The I.C. symbolizes personal growth and integration. A synthesis of this angle with the phase arc of Jupiter and Saturn results in a part that points to the experiences that one may most readily use as a foundation for the individualized perspective and inspiration necessary for a meaningful relationship with society or a collective unit. This point also represents the internalization of one's experiences with society and how one can best fulfill their potential in a manner beneficial to both one's self and one's society.

THE PART OF JUPITER-SATURN AND THE M.C.

Formula: M.C.+Jupiter-Saturn phase arc

This point occupies the degree of the zodiac opposite the above part. It is derived from the M.C., and is therefore connected with one's social and spiritual functions. The house and sign occupied by this part reveal the area of experience and the type of energy through which one may most readily realize his or her place and function in society (and on a larger scale, his or her relationship to the universe) as a unqiue individual. It points to the ways in which one may discover and fulfill his or her spiritual identity through the synthesis of individual purpose and a social, cultural, or planetary need.

Part Three

SYNASTRY: A GUIDE TO
UNDERSTANDING RELATIONSHIP

9. THE TECHNIQUES OF SYNASTRY

This chapter introduces the philosophical and practical implications of various synastric techniques: zodiacal contact charts, house contact charts, house transposition charts, composites, and progressions and transits. The use and interpretation of synastric charts is illustrated in Chapter 10. Guides to the construction of the various charts (all of which are derived from conventional birth charts) are included here as well as some suggested procedures for organizing and tabulating their significant features.

BIRTH CHARTS

The first step in the synastric procedure is the construction and interpretation of the birth charts of the individuals involved in the relationship under consideration. I have discussed the details of casting and interpreting birth charts at length in *A Handbook for the Humanistic Astrologer*. We touched on the significance of birth charts in Part One; here we will show how the vital symbolic information contained within them can be effectively organized and tabulated to aid the interpretative process and how various synastric charts derived from natal factors can be constructed.

ZODIACAL CONTACTS

The zodiac is an astrological frame of reference composed of twelve signs that symbolize twelve archetypal qualities of collective human nature and energy utilization. The astrological zodiac is what astronomers refer to as the *ecliptic of the zodiac*, a phenomenon produced by the *apparent* annual path of the sun as it is observed from the Earth. As we explained in Part Two, this zodiac of signs, or the ecliptic, is often confused with the zodiac of constellations which is an entirely different frame of reference not extensively used by most astrologers.

All objects in the geocentric sky have a position somewhere along the zodiac, a zodiacal longitude between 0 and 360 degrees. The distance between two planets in terms of zodiacal longitude determines their aspect or phase arc. For example, when one planet is positioned at 0° Aries and another is at 0° Gemini, they are forming a sextile aspect, a phase arc of sixty degrees.

The most commonly used technique of synastry is the study of the zodiacal aspects or contacts between the natal planets and angles of two (or more) persons. If the zodiacal position of Mars in one person's chart is ninety degrees (a square aspect) from the zodiacal position of another's natal Venus, for instance, there should be a powerful, possibly confrontative but potentially constructive, energy circulating and vitalizing their relationship. Since the configuration involves the planets Mars and Venus, it could help the individuals reach a better understanding of their personal values, emotions, feelings, or sexuality.

Zodiacal contacts between the charts of two persons can tell us something about the type of relationship existing between the two individuals in terms of the general nature, temperament, and energy symbolized by the two planets involved. It can reveal something about the energy flow between the two persons, suggest the way their temperaments might blend, indicate whether there is a potential for strong attraction or repulsion, or reveal areas of particular harmony or conflict between the particular functions symbolized by the planets. In the instance of a Mars-Venus square we could expect a strong physical, emotional, sexual attraction or repulsion.

There is a limitation, however, in dealing strictly with zodiacal references: They reveal very little about ways in which the energies represented by zodiacal contacts can best be released, through what experiences they can best operate and establish themselves; how, in short, the individuals can best use the dynamic energies generated by their relationship. In order to reach some basic understanding of these processes, we need to study the two charts in reference to the circle of houses. A method for doing this is presented in the following section of this chapter.

In spite of this limitation, a consideration of the zodiacal contacts existing between birth charts is an appropriate way to begin practical synastric studies. It is the zodiacal energies that are usually most apparent in personalities. People most often form relationships with one another not necessarily because they have established a ground of common or complementary experience, but because they are attracted to one another's general quality of energy, temperament, vibrations, and appearance, and the way their energies blend and flow with one another. Interpersonal contacts, then, are usually made initially on the zodiacal level through an attraction or repulsion of energies. Afterward the partners may begin to channel their energies toward sharing the achievement of mutual purposes and experiences (symbolized by the houses).

The zodiacal aspects existing between the natal planets and angles of two or more birth charts can be organized and made apparent by drawing up a *zodiacal contact chart*. In such a chart the zodiac is the fixed frame of reference with the persons' natal planets and angles placed within its structure—making it possible to see both sets of natal factors relative to the same zodiacal background, on one piece of paper (see chart on page 201). Zodiacal contact charts are discussed extensively in the following chapter, along with the other synastric charts presented below.

HOW TO CONSTRUCT A ZODIACAL CONTACT CHART

The zodiacal contact chart is an easily constructed aid in the comparison of two or more birth charts. It is simply a chart divided into twelve sections, one for each sign, with the individuals' natal factors arranged around it, in concentric circles, according to their zodiacal positions. I have found it convenient to always use the inner circle for the older person. The chart on page 201 illustrates.

To determine aspects and phase arcs between the individual sets of natal factors, one simply calculates the distance between the positions on one concentric circle and the factors of the other person, situated on the next circle. For instance, Freud's natal sun is 16°21′ Taurus (46°21′), Jung's natal sun is 3°19′ Leo (123°19′); the arc between the two is 76°58′ (123°19′−46°21′=76°58′).

It is helpful to tabulate the various phase arcs existing between the two sets of natal factors for easy reference. The conventional way to measure these arcs is to simply calculate the distance between two planets in terms of their nearest arc. This procedure, however, overlooks the cyclic character of planetary motions. The most apparent remedy for this inadequacy is, when calculating the arcs between two sets of natal factors, to use the distance from the older person's factors to the younger's, taken in a counterclockwise direction. By doing this we recognize the natural dynamic flow of planetary cycles and can achieve a clearer understanding of planetary aspects operating through a particular planetary contact, especially in terms of the waxing and waning hemicycles.

For instance, turning to the Freud-Jung zodiacal contact chart, notice that Freud's natal Saturn is 27°33′ Gemini (87°33′) while Jung's natal Saturn occupies 24°13′ Aquarius (324°13′). Since Freud was born several years before Jung, to find the cyclic arc between their Saturns we would want to calculate the distance between 87°33′ and 324°13′ which is 236°40′ (324°13′−87°33′= 236°40′). This is a waning/applying trine with a 3°20′ orb. In the time between the births of Freud and Jung the planet Saturn completed just under two-thirds of its twenty-eight-year cycle.

The moon transits the zodiac much faster than Saturn (completing one zodiacal cycle every 27.32 days). The cyclic arc between

Freud's moon (14°44′ Gemini) and Jung's natal moon (15°28′ Taurus) is 330°44′. We see then that the two moons form a waning separating semi-sextile. During the interval between the two births the moon transited the zodiac 123 times and was just about to complete its 124th round.

HOUSE CONTACTS AND HOUSE TRANSPOSITION

The circle of twelve houses is the most individualized astrological frame of reference. It symbolizes the most particular qualities of experience, selfhood, and relatedness, while the zodiac represents qualities of a more collective and general nature. The planet Jupiter, for instance, occupies a certain degree of the zodiac, say the tenth degree of Aries, for a week or so before it moves into the following degree. Everyone born during that one-week period has Jupiter in the same zodiacal position in their natal charts. Jupiter (or any planet), on the other hand, moves through the entire cycle of twelve houses (360 degrees) every twenty-four hours since the houses reflect the daily rotation of the earth on its axis.

In a natal chart the houses represent twelve archetypal areas of individual experience: the experience of emerging into the realm of conscious being (first house), the experience of substantiating the self (second house), the experience of interacting with the environment (third house), and so on. As a frame of reference in synastry, the houses refer to twelve types of mutual experience; the experience of recognizing or initiating a relationship, the experience of giving substance and form to the relationship, the experience of collective interaction with the environment, and so on.

Many astrologers tend to give more attention to the zodiacal positions of the planets than to their places in the houses. Humanistic astrologers, however, are more concerned with individual potentialities and development than with collective pressures, external events, and the like. Events and social factors are, of course, important, but from a humanistic, transpersonal perspective, their true significance is in terms of the person who is experiencing them. It is mainly for this reason that the humanistic astrologer studies the houses extensively.

HOUSE CONTACT CHARTS

The house contact chart, one of two house-oriented synastric techniques I would like to introduce here, provides valuable insight into the meaning of a relationship on the level of mutual experience, as well as suggesting how each individual may experience the relationship itself. Such a chart emphasizes the houses, using them as its fixed structure. It clearly illustrates the individuals' planetary gestalts and their combination, in addition to making apparent planetary aspects between natal positions within the context of the circle of houses. If, for instance, my moon is exactly in the middle of my ninth house and another person's sun is exactly in the middle of his or her third house, the two bodies are exactly opposite in terms of the circle of houses, regardless of their zodiacal location.

The house contact chart contains identical natal positions to the zodiacal contact chart, but the orientation of the individual natal patterns within differ between the two. In the zodiacal contact chart, the planets, etc., of both individuals are oriented according to their positions in terms of the first degree of the zodiac (0° Aries) —regardless of their house positions. Conversely, in the house contact chart, both sets of natal factors are oriented in terms of their relation to the individuals' natal ascendants, regardless of zodiacal placement.

A comparison of the house contact chart with the zodiacal contact chart can uncover further threads in the web of the relationship: If one's natal Mars, for instance, is 19 degrees Leo and another's Venus is in the nineteenth segment of the fifth house, both planetary functions are at the same phase of development—the Martian function on the level of energy, and the Venusian along the lines of experience. One's way of using externalizing, mobilizing energies is similar to the other's manner of achieving the experience of inner harmony and appreciation.

HOUSE TRANSPOSITION CHARTS

A second house-oriented synastric technique involves the construction and interpretation of house transposition charts. The house contact chart can be seen as a map describing mutual and complementary fields of experience. The house transposition chart is constructed by placing the natal planets of one person into the house structure of another's birth chart. It complements the symbolism of the house contact chart by revealing how one person experiences and best reponds to another. If my natal moon falls into the fifth house of another's chart, for instance, his or her urge toward the experience of creative self-expression (fifth house) should be stimulated through being exposed to my particular manner of expression, to my way of handling the demands of daily living and adapting to a particular situation (moon). The type of energy integrated in the experience depends largely on the zodiacal sign involved of the planet under consideration.

HOW TO CONSTRUCT THE HOUSE CONTACT CHART

The house contact chart is based on the same concept as the zodiacal contact chart, only it is structured by the houses rather than the zodiac. That is, the relative house positions of two or more sets of natal planets, regardless of their zodiacal positions, are superimposed upon each other, as illustrated on page 204. This chart makes apparent the arcs or phases existing between planets from a house-oriented perspective. For instance, even though the zodiacal arc between Freud's and Jung's natal suns is almost 46 degrees, from a house orientation they occupy nearly the same part of the seventh house. That is, they form a house-oriented conjunction indicating that the two should fulfill their individual purposes through very much the same type of experiences, although the modes of energy used in the effort may be distinctly different. The house arcs existing between the two sets of natal planets can be tabulated in much the same way as the phase arcs in the zodiacal contact chart.

There is a limitation in the house contact chart: Accurately timed or rectified birth charts are essential. Because about one degree passes over the ascendant every four minutes, an error of more than a few minutes will produce many discrepancies. For this reason it is not advisable to construct a house contact chart unless both birth times are known to be accurate within eight or twelve minutes.

Since different houses within the same chart usually contain varying number of zodiacal degrees, it is necessary to convert to a standard measure of thirty units per house to achieve correspondence. One house may span 26 degrees of the zodiac while another encloses 34 degrees; when comparing the house positions with another's chart, we may find 40 degrees in one house and only 20 zodiacal degrees in another. In order to conveniently calculate cross references, it is necessary to relate the proportions to a standard measure. Since the standard measure in astrology is 360 degrees divided into twelve sections of 30 degrees, it would seem logical to adopt a measure of 30 units for this purpose.

The following formula can be used to implement such conversions.

1. Calculate the number of zodiacal degrees and minutes in each house.

2. Calculate the number of zodiacal degrees and minutes between each planet and the cusp of the house it occupies. For example, there are 26 degrees in Freud's sixth house ($12°$ Aries to $8°$ Taurus). The planet Venus, at $26°10'$ Aries, is $14°10'$ from the sixth house cusp.

3. Calculate the house-oriented position by the formula:
$$\frac{\text{degrees from cusp to planet}}{\text{degrees in house}} \times 30.$$

In our example: $\frac{14°10'}{26°} \times 30 = \frac{850'}{1560'} \times 30 = 16.3$

Venus is located in the 16th of 30 units in the sixth house.

The House Degree Conversion Table on the following pages can be used as an alternative to calculating by this formula. To use it find the column at the head that is nearest to the number of degrees in the particular house. Read down that column to the number that is nearest to the zodiacal arc between the cusp and the planet's position. Once this number is located, read across to the extreme left column on the same horizontal line. This is the house position of the planet reproportioned to a scale of 0–30 units regardless of the number of zodiacal degrees in the house. Freud's sixth house contains 26 degrees and his Venus is 14°10′ from the sixth house cusp. It is located in the 16th, of 30 units of the sixth house. Greater accuracy can be achieved by interpolating.

It is easy and perhaps more accurate to reproportion house positions with an electronic calculator. If you are using a calculator, you will need to convert all minutes of arc to decimals. The conversion table below serves this purpose.

DECIMAL EQUIVALENTS OF MINUTES

1- .02	21- .35	41- .68
2- .03	22- .37	42- .70
3- .05	23- .38	43- .72
4- .07	24- .40	44- .73
5- .08	25- .42	45- .75
6- .10	26- .43	46- .77
7- .12	27- .45	47- .78
8- .13	28- .47	48- .80
9- .15	29- .48	49- .82
10- .17	30- .50	50- .83
11- .18	31- .52	51- .85
12- .20	32- .53	52- .87
13- .22	33- .55	53- .88
14- .23	34- .57	54- .90
15- .25	35- .58	55- .92
16- .27	36- .60	56- .93
17- .28	37- .62	57- .95
18- .30	38- .63	58- .97
19- .32	39- .65	59- .98
20- .33	40- .67	60- 1.00

HOUSE DEGREE CONVERSION TABLE

	20	21	22	23	24
0	0:0	0:0	0:0	0:0	0:0
1	0:40	0:42	0:44	0:46	0:48
2	1:20	1:24	1:28	1:32	1:36
3	2:00	2:06	2:12	2:18	2:24
4	2:40	2:48	2:56	3:04	3:12
5	3:20	3:30	3:40	3:50	4:00
6	4:00	4:12	4:24	4:36	4:48
7	4:40	4:54	5:08	5:22	5:36
8	5:20	5:36	5:52	6:08	6:24
9	6:00	6:18	6:36	6:54	7:12
10	6:40	7:00	7:20	7:40	8:00
11	7:20	7:42	8:04	8:26	8:48
12	8:00	8:24	8:48	9:12	9:36
13	8:40	9:06	9:32	9:58	10:24
14	9:20	9:48	10:16	10:44	11:12
15	10:00	10:30	11:00	11:30	12:00
16	10:40	11:12	11:44	12:16	12:48
17	11:20	11:54	12:28	13:02	13:36
18	12:00	12:36	13:12	13:48	12:24
19	12:40	13:18	13:56	14:34	15:12
20	13:20	14:00	14:40	15:20	16:00
21	14:00	14:42	15:24	16:06	16:48
22	14:40	15:24	16:08	16:52	17:36
23	15:20	16:06	16:52	17:38	18:24
24	16:00	16:48	17:36	18:24	19:12
25	16:40	17:30	18:20	19:10	20:00
26	17:20	18:12	19:04	19:56	20:48
27	18:00	18:54	19:48	20:42	21:36
28	18:40	19:36	20:32	21:28	21:24
29	19:20	20:18	21:16	22:14	23:12
	60	63	66	69	72

HOUSE DEGREE CONVERSION TABLE

	25	26	27	28	29	30
0	0:0	0:0	0:0	0:0	0:0	0:0
1	0:50	0:52	0:54	0:56	0:58	1:0
2	1:40	1:44	1:48	1:52	1:56	2:0
3	2:30	2:36	2:42	2:48	2:54	3:0
4	3:20	3:28	3:36	3:44	3:52	4:0
5	4:10	4:20	4:30	4:40	4:50	5:0
6	5:00	5:12	5:24	5:36	5:48	6:0
7	5:50	6:04	6:18	6:32	6:46	7:0
8	6:40	6:56	7:12	7:28	7:44	8:0
9	7:30	7:48	8:06	8:24	8:42	9:0
10	8:20	8:40	9:00	9:20	9:40	10:0
11	9:10	9:32	9:54	10:16	10:38	11:0
12	10:00	10:24	10:48	11:12	11:36	12:0
13	10:50	11:16	11:42	12:08	12:34	13:0
14	11:40	12:08	12:36	13:04	13:32	14:0
15	12:30	13:00	13:30	14:00	14:30	15:0
16	13:20	13:52	14:24	14:56	15:28	16:0
17	14:10	14:44	15:18	15:52	16:26	17:0
18	15:00	15:36	16:12	16:48	17:24	18:0
19	15:50	16:28	17:06	17:44	18:22	19:0
20	16:40	17:20	18:00	18:40	19:20	20:0
21	17:30	18:12	18:54	19:36	20:18	21:0
22	18:20	19:04	19:48	20:32	21:16	22:0
23	19:10	19:56	20:42	21:28	22:14	23:0
24	20:00	20:48	21:36	22:24	23:12	24:0
25	20:50	21:40	22:30	23:20	24:10	25:0
26	21:40	22:32	23:24	24:16	25:08	26:0
27	22:30	23:24	24:18	25:12	26:06	27:0
28	23:20	24:16	25:12	26:08	27:04	28:0
29	24:10	25:08	26:06	27:04	28:02	29:0
	75	78	81	84	87	90

HOUSE DEGREE CONVERSION TABLE

	31	32	33	34	35
0	0:0	0:0	0:0	0:0	0:0
1	1:02	1:04	1:06	1:08	1:10
2	2:04	2:08	2:12	2:16	2:20
3	3:06	3:12	3:18	3:24	3:30
4	4:08	4:16	4:24	4:32	4:40
5	5:10	5:20	5:30	5:40	5:50
6	6:12	6:24	6:36	6:48	7:00
7	7:14	7:28	7:42	7:56	8:10
8	8:16	8:32	8:48	9:04	9:20
9	9:18	9:36	9:54	10:12	10:30
10	10:20	10:40	11:00	11:20	11:40
11	11:22	11:44	12:06	12:28	12:50
12	12:24	12:48	13:12	13:36	14:00
13	13:26	13:52	14:18	14:44	15:10
14	14:28	14:56	15:24	15:52	16:20
15	15:30	16:00	16:30	17:00	17:30
16	16:32	17:04	17:36	18:08	18:40
17	17:34	18:08	18:42	19:16	19:50
18	18:36	19:12	19:48	20:24	21:00
19	19:38	20:16	20:54	21:32	22:10
20	20:40	21:20	21:00	22:40	23:20
21	21:42	22:24	23:06	23:48	24:30
22	22:44	23:28	24:12	24:56	25:40
23	23:46	24:32	25:18	26:04	26:50
24	24:48	25:36	26:24	27:12	28:00
25	25:50	26:40	27:30	28:20	29:10
26	26:52	27:44	28:36	29:28	30:20
27	27:54	28:48	29:42	30:36	31:30
28	28:56	29:52	30:48	31:44	32:40
29	29:58	30:56	31:54	32:52	33:50
	93	96	99	102	105

HOUSE DEGREE CONVERSION TABLE

	36	37	38	39	40	41
0	0:0	0:0	0:0	0:0	0:0	0:0
1	1:12	1:14	1:16	1:18	1:20	1:22
2	2:24	2:28	2:32	2:36	2:40	2:44
3	3:36	3:42	3:48	3:54	4:00	4:06
4	4:48	4:56	5:04	5:12	5:20	5:28
5	6:00	6:10	6:20	6:30	6:40	6:50
6	7:12	7:24	7:36	7:48	8:00	8:12
7	8:24	8:38	8:52	9:06	9:20	9:34
8	9:36	9:52	10:08	10:24	10:40	10:56
9	10:48	11:06	11:24	11:42	12:00	12:18
10	12:00	12:20	12:40	13:00	13:20	13:40
11	13:12	13:34	13:56	14:18	14:40	15:02
12	14:24	14:48	15:12	15:36	16:00	16:24
13	15:36	16:02	16:28	16:54	17:20	17:46
14	16:48	17:16	17:44	18:12	18:40	19:08
15	18:00	18:30	19:00	19:30	20:00	20:30
16	19:12	19:44	20:16	20:48	21:20	21:52
17	20:24	20:58	21:32	22:06	22:40	23:12
18	21:36	22:12	22:48	23:24	24:00	24:36
19	22:48	23:26	24:04	24:42	25:20	25:58
20	24:00	24:40	25:20	26:00	26:40	27:20
21	25:12	25:54	26:36	27:18	28:00	28:42
22	26:24	27:08	27:52	28:36	29:20	30:04
23	27:36	28:22	39:08	29:54	30:40	31:26
24	28:48	29:36	30:24	31:12	32:00	32:48
25	30:00	30:50	31:40	32:30	33:20	34:10
26	31:12	32:04	32:56	33:48	34:40	35:32
27	32:24	33:18	34:12	35:06	36:00	36:54
28	33:36	34:32	35:28	36:20	37:20	38:16
29	34:48	35:46	36:44	37:48	38:40	39:38
	108	**111**	**114**	**117**	**120**	**123**

COMPOSITE CHARTS

A composite chart is a chart composed of the mutual zodiacal midpoints of two or more birth charts. For instance, if my natal sun is thirteen degrees Scorpio and another's natal sun is thirteen degrees Capricorn, our composite sun is thirteen Sagittarius (exactly midway between thirteen Scorpio and thirteen Capricorn). While conventional composite charts are based on zodiacal midpoints alone, a thorough analysis may include the construction of a composite chart based on house-oriented midpoints as well.

Composite charts can reveal how the energies (zodiacal composites) and experiences (house-oriented composites) of the individuals can be best balanced, synthesized, and mutually released or channeled. A composite chart can be understood as a chart of the relationship, revealing its quality and focal areas more or less independently of the personal perspectives of the individuals involved. It is a map describing the various qualities, potentialities, temperament, etc. of the relationship itself. Compared with the birth charts of the individuals involved, an understanding may be reached of how each can best approach this relationship.

HOW TO CONSTRUCT COMPOSITE CHARTS

A composite chart is a synthesis of elements and is purely symbolic—the planets so positioned may never actually appear that way in reality. To calculate a composite chart we simply find the zodiacal midpoint between a planet in one person's chart and the same planet in the chart of another. For instance, Freud's natal sun is 16°21′ Taurus while Jung's is 3°18′ Leo. Their composite sun is then 24°50′ Gemini (see chart on page 209).

Conventionally, astrologers have simply calculated the midpoint between the two bodies in the direction of their nearest arc. It is more in keeping with the cyclic orientation of humanistic astrology, however, to calculate composite planets with a consciousness of phase. To accomplish this, we should divide the arc between the two planets in the direction of their natural motion—from the position of the older person's planets to the younger's in terms of the planets' paths through the zodiac from Aries to Pisces. Not every planet is different in a composite chart calculated by this method in comparison to one calculated according to the conventional nearest arc method. Differences occur only when the phase arc between the two planets exceeds 180 degrees. In such instances the cyclic composite planet will occupy a position directly opposite that calculated by the nearest arc method. Midpoints are actually the poles of an axis.

The following procedure may be used to calculate composite planets according to both methods.

The nearest arc method always *adds* the zodiacal longitudes of the two natal bodies and divides the result by two.

$$74°44' \quad (14°44' \text{ Gemini}) \text{ Freud's moon}$$
$$+ \ 45°28' \quad (15°28' \text{ Taurus}) \text{ Jung's moon}$$
$$\overline{120°12'}$$
$$120°12' \quad \div 2 = 60°06' \ (0°06' \text{ Gemini}) \text{ composite moon}$$

The cyclic or phase arc method follows the same procedure as above, except the longitude of the younger person's planet must always be greater than the older's—if it is not, 360 should be added before the division.

$$74°44' \quad (14°44') \text{ Freud's moon}$$
$$45°28' \quad (15°28') \text{ Jung's moon}$$
$$+360°00' \quad \text{adjustment}$$
$$\overline{480°12'}$$
$$480°12' \quad \div 2 + 240°06' \ (0°06' \text{ Sagittarius}) \text{ composite moon.}$$

The composite angles may be calculated in a similar fashion. Freud's M.C., for instance, is 20° Leo; Jung's is 26° Scorpio—their composite M.C. is 8° Libra. The same may be done with the ascendant. If both individuals are living on or near the same geographic latitude, it may be best to calculate only the composite M.C. and refer to a table of houses for the local composite ascendant and house cusps that correspond to the composite M.C. at that particular latitude.

MULTIPLE COMPOSITES

Composite charts can be drawn up for a relationship involving more than two individuals. There are several ways in which to approach this. For three individuals we might construct three composites, each focusing on a particular couple within the relationship. Or, given three natal charts, A, B, and C, we can set up one composite between the charts of A and B and a second fusing the A-B composite with C's natal chart—emphasizing the A-B relationship and revealing how C fits into this particular orientation. A third could be constructed relating A's and C's birth charts with a fourth (focusing on the A-C orientation) created by combining the A-C composite with B's chart. The natal charts of B and C could be synthesized to give us a fifth, and that one with A's for a sixth that gives special attention to the B-C aspect of the triadic relationship.

HOUSE-ORIENTED COMPOSITES

Conventional composites are constructed from zodiacal midpoints and thus emphasize zodiacal characteristics. It is also possible to use the house positions of the natal planets for the construction of composites that focus on the circle of houses and the qualities of experience the houses symbolize.

The construction of these charts is identical with that outlined above for the zodiacal-oriented composites, except that house positions are used in place of zodiacal positions. Also, while zodiacal composites do include composite angles, house-oriented composites do not include zodiacal references.

Here are some examples:

$$
\begin{array}{ll}
166{:}21 & (16{:}21 \text{ of the sixth) Freud's Venus} \\
+164{:}45 & (14{:}45 \text{ of the sixth) Jung's Venus} \\
\hline
331{:}06 & \div 2 = 165{:}33 \ (15{:}33 \text{ of the sixth) composite Venus.}
\end{array}
$$

```
 212:25   (2:25 of the eighth) Freud's moon
  51:58   (21:58 of the second) Jung's moon
+360:00   adjustment
─────────
 624:23   ÷2=312:12 (12:12 of the eleventh) composite moon.
```

PROGRESSIONS AND TRANSITS

A person's pattern of being is represented by his or her birth chart. Astrological progressions reveal one's pattern or cycle of becoming. That is, natal factors symbolize birth potentials; progressions demonstrate how those potentials can become fulfilled. By studying the positions of the planets as they progress through the signs and houses of the natal chart, constantly changing their angular relationships with natal positions as well as other chart factors, we can better understand what transformations may be called for in order for one to evolve as an individual, fulfilling his or her birth potential.

Astrologers use several methods to progress natal factors, each valid, but each applying to a certain realm of existence or activity in that they employ different frames of reference. The two methods I have chosen to present here are the one-day to one-year method of secondary progressions and the one-degree to one-year system of direction.*

Secondary progressions focus on the gradual development of the functions represented by the planets within the psyche of the individual. Degree-to-year directions (some astrologers may prefer what is known as "solar arc" directions to this method) emphasize the archetypal solar factor of personality and its utilization in multifunctional activities. When using secondary progressions we progress all the planets at their own rate of motions, equating one day of such motion with one year of life. The planets' positions twenty

---

* Directions are a special type of "progression": All natal factors are advanced at the same rate in systems of direction, whereas progressions use the actual daily motion of each planet, the various systems equating their motions with different spans of time in an individual's growth.

days after one was born represent one's twentieth year of life. On the other hand, degree-to-year directions progress all natal factors at a rate of one degree (the solar archetype) to one year of growth, thus placing more attention on the solar function than do the secondary progressions.

Transits are the current planetary positions, representing external conditions that can serve as channels for the expression of natal or progressed configurations. They are quite distinct from progressions in terms of meaning: progressions symbolize the gradual development and emergence of internal potentials while transits represent the external, social, and collective circumstances prevailing at the time.

From a synastric perspective, directions and transits can be compared not only with one's own natal chart, revealing the opportunities for growth at a particular time, but also with another's natal chart and with various synastric charts. When, for instance, my progressed Venus is conjunct another's natal Venus, it could be said —on one of many possible levels of meaning—that my function of appreciation, internalization, and receptivity or, from a Jungian point of view, my *anima*, should have unfolded to the point where it is in union with the same type of energy or experience being focused through the other's natal Venus. In other words, in terms of the Venusian function, there should be a mutual identification between myself and the other person.

HOW TO CALCULATE PROGRESSIONS, DIRECTIONS, AND TRANSITS

Secondary progressions are based on the symbolic relationship between a day of objective time and a year of subjective growth. To calculate secondary progressions, an ephemeris is needed that extends as many days after birth as the year of age for which one wishes to progress the natal planets. One year in this system equals twenty-four hours, one month of life equals two hours in the ephemeris, and one day equals four minutes.

The progressed date and time for a person twenty-seven years and nine months of age is found by adding an increment of 27 days and 18 hours to his or her birth date and Greenwich Mean Time. The exact progressed positions have to be interpolated to the exact progressed GMT, unless the GMT turns out to be very close to midnight (if one is using a midnight ephemeris) or noon (if one is using a noon ephemeris).

Degree-year or one-degree directions relate one year of life to one zodiacal degree. The one-degree measure is implemented by simply adding one degree to the natal positions for each year of life, five minutes of an arc for each month, and ten seconds of an arc for each day. For example, if a person is thirty-four years, five months, and four days of age, his one-degree directions are found by adding 34 degrees 25 minutes and 40 seconds of arc to the position of each planet.

Transits are the current day-to-day positions of the planets and can be calculated from an ephemeris for the current year and related to the natal and progressed positions of the planets and angles.†

GUIDELINES TO SYNASTRIC INTERPRETATION

Synastry can be an effective astrological tool for gaining a clearer understanding of the nature and potentiality of relationships of both horizontal and vertical types. That is, synastry can be used to analyze a relationship between two or more persons on a person-to-person level or to analyze a relationship existing, for instance, between a country and a city, a city and a person who resides in it, or a corporation and its administrator.

The many synastric techniques presented in the following pages are all applied to birth charts of individuals engaged in relationship. Birth charts not only represent seeds of individuality, the focus of our being, but also the foundation of relatedness: Relationship is the linking of centers.

† A more detailed explanation of progressions and transits, as well as many useful tables, can be found in *A Handbook for the Humanistic Astrologer*.

This volume gives a great many different synastric techniques, all of which are valuable, though each represents a different aspect of relationship. When working with these techniques it is always best to proceed along orderly lines rather than jumping chaotically from one line of inquiry to another. The procedure given below has been most useful to me when working with chart comparison, though in many instances it may not be practical or necessary to complete the entire process.

1. A study of the birth charts on an individual basis. Regardless of how many of the numerous synastric techniques one puts a pair of charts through, the end results can only be as comprehensive as one's understanding of the individuals on singular terms.

2. A comparison of the two (or more) zodiacal contact charts in terms of aspects, elements, modes, etc.

3. A comparison of the house-oriented contact charts from the perspective of their planetary gestalts, house-oriented aspects, etc.

4. A comparison of the zodiacal contact chart with the house contact chart.

5. The construction and interpretation of a composite chart.

6. A comparison of the progressed positions of the birth charts to the positions of the factors composing the various synastric charts. A consideration of the transiting planetary positions in terms of the natal and synastric charts and their progressions.

7. A consideration of other factors that might be of significance; such as the chart of the city where the individuals reside, their relocational charts, the chart of the time and place of their first meeting, etc.

THE PRACTICE OF SYNASTRY

I have chosen to explore three relationships on the following pages to demonstrate an application of the various synastric techniques outlined in the preceding chapter. First, we will look at the relationship between Sigmund Freud and C. G. Jung, which demonstrates two individuals working together professionally for the purpose of expanding and transforming some traditional concepts of human consciousness. Second, the study of the birth and synastric charts of George Sand, the renowned French novelist and one of the very first modern liberated women, and Frederic Chopin, with whom she lived and worked for several years, examines a romantic male-female union having deep creative and cultural implications. Finally, we will look into a relationship in which two individuals— H. P. Blavatsky and her executive collaborator, Henry Olcott— worked together under most unusual conditions for the fulfillment of what they believed to be a great spiritual-planetary task.

As one studies astrological charts or reads interpretations of charts such as those included in this chapter, it is important to keep in mind the fact that astrological symbolism can be applied with equal validity on a variety of levels. Just as algebraic calculations can be applied in terms of engineering, physics, mathematics, chemistry, etc., the same astrological chart can be employed in terms of health, personal psychology, vocation, relationship, spiritual guidance, and a great many other perspectives. Even those of us who study charts from a similar orientation or for a common purpose have our own individual understanding of astrological symbolism. The discussions of the following charts are by no means exhaustive; the search for the meaning of the symbolism of one chart, as it can be understood on all possible levels, is an endless process. I have attempted here to present the reader with several interesting birth and synastric charts along with brief interpretations of their most evident characteristics as a means of demonstrating a procedure for working along synastric lines. Extensive tabulations are included with each chart as an aid to those wishing to probe these or other relationships more deeply.

SIGMUND FREUD AND C. G. JUNG

SIGMUND FREUD: A NATAL PERSPECTIVE

Sigmund Freud, the founder of psychoanalysis, was born on May 6, 1856, in Freiberg, Moravia, at 6:30 P.M. local mean time. The upper portion of the accompanying figure is the birth chart of Sigmund Freud. The grid of numbers directly below the chart is composed of the following elements.

1. The small numerals directly below the horizontally arranged planetary symbols are the zodiacal positions of the planets expressed in terms of degrees (0–360) and minutes (0–60) of longitude. Freud's natal Saturn is located, for instance, at 87°33′, or 27°33′ Gemini.

2. The numbers that are listed in the table below the planetary positions and above the diagonal space are the phase arcs existing between the forty-five planetary pairs. The numbers express phase arcs only in terms of degrees and not minutes of arc. The phase arcs are rounded off to the next nearest whole degree (an arc anywhere between 10°01′ to 11° is represented as 11°). The phase arc between Freud's Mercury and Jupiter, for example, is 59°.

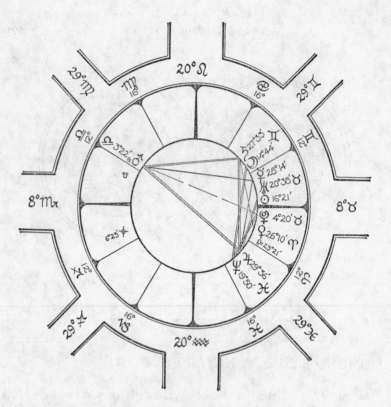

Sigmund Freud's Birth Chart

	☉ 46°21'	☽ 74°44'	☿ 58°14'	♀ 26°10'	♂ 183°22'	♃ 359°36'	♄ 87°35'	♅ 50°38'	♆ 349°50'	♇ 34°20'
☉ 187:22		29	12	340	223	47	319	356	57	13
☽ 212:25	26		17	49	252	76	348	25	85	41
☿ 197:51	11	15		33	235	59	331	8	69	24
♀ 166:21	339	47	32		203	27	299	336	37	352
♂ 320:3	228	253	238	207		184	96	133	194	150
♃ 135:41	52	77	63	31	185		273	309	10	326
♄ 223:43	324	349	335	303	97	272		37	98	54
♅ 191:9	357	22	7	336	129	305	33		61	17
♆ 124:25	63	88	74	42	196	12	100	67		316
♇ 175:46	12	37	23	351	145	320	48	16	309	

3. The numbers directly to the right of the vertical line of planetary symbols are the house-oriented positions of the planets. The
house-oriented position of Freud's natal Saturn is, for instance,
223:43.

4. The numerals in the wedge that extends to the right of the
house-oriented positions and to the left of the diagonal space are the
house-oriented phase arcs. The house-oriented phase arc between
Freud's Mars and Uranus is 129°.

The single most outstanding feature of Freud's birth chart is its
bucket, or funnel, planetary pattern—a gestalt where all but one
planet are condensed within a space of three or four houses, the singleton being distinctly separate from this group. Mars, retrograde at
the time of Freud's birth, plays the role of singleton, acting as a
channel for the release, or, as Freud would say, catharsis, of a single-
pointed outflow of dynamism generated by the other nine planets.
The energies and experiences generated by the main group of
planets can be understood by the group's orientation in terms of the
zodiac and houses. Neptune (the planet symbolizing the transcendental, universalizing element of life, and psychoanalysis) in the
fifth house of creative self-expression and in the sign it naturally
rules, Pisces, is 98 zodiacal degrees from Saturn (symbol of form,
structure, and definition) in the eighth house of interpersonal exchange and in the associative sign of Gemini. The midpoint axis of
these two planets serves as a focus or pivot for the energies
generated by the entire group of planets they enclose. This center
of gravity extends from 8°41′ Taurus to 8°41′ Scorpio—lining up
almost exactly on Freud's natal horizon, placing great emphasis on
his individual "line of awareness" (the horizon). The relatedness
pole of the horizon (the descendant) is surrounded by the nine
planets, naturally stimulating Freud's awareness of and interest in
relationship, while the selfhood (ascendant) pole is somewhat remote from planetary contact. These factors reflect the central importance Freud placed on sexuality and its varied implications in the
development of his psychoanalytic theories.

The Sabian symbol for the center of gravity for the grouping of
nine planets sheds light on Freud's ability to utilize his energies for
the assistance of others. The symbol for 8°41′ (the ninth degree according to the Sabian system) Taurus, in Dane Rudhyar's *An As-*

trological Mandala, reads: "*A fully decorated Christmas tree.*"
Rudhyar gives a keynote of "the ability to create inner happiness in
dark hours" to this symbol, speaking directly to the aim of psychoanalytic practice.

The singleton in a funnel pattern represents an extremely emphasized area of the psyche. In Freud's natal map, Mars retrograde is
singleton in the eleventh house, in the fourth degree of Libra. Since
this singleton Mars is in the eleventh house, the area of experience
through which Freud could best channel his intense drives (particularly symbolized by the stellium of four planets in Taurus and the
Scorpio-Taurus horizon) was the field of association with others on
the level of group integration, professional relations, and so on.
That Mars is also retrograde (outward action and motivation operating in a fashion that is "against the grain" of natural forces)
could, as do some other symbols here, represent Freud's aggressiveness in group situations and the professional difficulties his uncompromising attitude generated. The situation was probably com-
pounded by Mars being zodiacally positioned in the sign Libra,
giving Freud even more energy to participate in the field of relationship as well as having strong convictions in his own judgments.

The Sabian symbol for the house-oriented position (321°) of
Mars gives an idea of how Freud's powerful singleton Mars could
best operate as a dynamic release on the level of experience, as well
as how he may have personally experienced this distinctive funnel
configuration in the course of his professional career, ridden with
ostracism and conflicts. It reads: "*A disappointed and disillusioned
woman courageously faces a seemingly empty life*"; Rudhyar's
keynote for this symbol emphasizes "the capacity to meet emotionally upsetting experiences in human relationships with strength
of character and personal integrity."

The soli-lunar type is a significant symbol of how the most basic
bi-polar life forces are combined within an individual's personality.
In Freud's chart the soli-lunar arc is almost twenty-nine degrees;
during the new-moon phase. That is, although Freud was born
about two and a half days after the new moon, the next or crescent
phase did not begin until the soli-lunar arc reached 45° about three
and a half days after the new moon. The new-moon type represents
a personality that functions primarily in an instinctual fashion,

yearning for emergence. The lunation cycle is just beginning a new cycle of manifestation and only a small portion of its potential has emerged above the surface into the realm of consciousness. At the time of Freud's birth, the sun and moon were occupying the signs of Taurus and Gemini in the seventh and eighth houses respectively, a new-moon type functioning within the spheres of interaction with substance and the environment as well as in interpersonal contacts. In *The Lunation Cycle*, Rudhyar writes that the new-moon personality

> tends to be eminently subjective, impulsive and emotional in his responses to human relationship and social processes. This may produce a state of confusion, a tendency to project oneself upon others and the world at large, to live life and love as if they were dreams, or screens upon which to cast one's image— and often one's shadow. People and situations are met, in most cases, without much regard to what they actually are in *themselves;* they are symbols. [p. 50]

Another interesting configuration in Freud's chart is the T-cross linking Jupiter and singleton Mars by opposition with Saturn squaring both at the apex of the formation. A T-cross symbolizes a critical situation containing much constructive, even if confrontative, potential. This potential is further emphasized by the positions of all three of these planets in succedent, or focal, houses. The planet at the apex of a T-cross, Saturn in this instance, acts as an agent of synthesis playing a decisive role in bringing the triangle of energies together: Through its function, the awareness of the opposition can best be put to a constructive use if the conflicts implied by such a structure are to be integrated in a positive fashion. Freud's Mars-Jupiter opposition implies a strong sensitivity to social (Jupiter) drives (Mars) and the delicate interplay between individual expression (fifth house) and collective integration (eleventh house). It is difficult to speculate upon how successfully Freud was able to deal with such a configuration through a Saturnian function. Surely, he was at least partially successful. The dynamic represented by this T-cross may have found partial expression in Freud's overwhelming drive toward social achievement.

Potentialities may not always be actualized, or fully actualized. Even when actualization does take place, it may be manifest on various levels or in an incomplete manner. Individual temperaments and karma must come into consideration. Freud is recognized as a great pioneer, the founder of the psychoanalytic movement, although for many years his work was met with extreme criticism. Fixed signs on his natal angles represent his capacity for endurance in the face of adversity and ostracism. But he was so uncompromising about certain aspects of his teachings that, as Jung later implied, he appeared to value his personal authority as the originator and hierophant of psychoanalysis to the extent that he was unable to wholeheartedly promote a search for truth, a search that might eventually overthrow his own established theories. It was these qualities in Freud's personality that led to the frustration and eventual breakdown of associations between him and most of his creative followers, including Jung, Adler, Assagioli, and Reich. In astrological symbolism this pride of authority and the "right to be right" is an expression of the negative side of the principle of fixity (represented by the zodiacal signs of Taurus, Leo, Scorpio, and Aquarius, and the second, fifth, eighth, and eleventh houses).

Freud's mission, in any case, which he of course fulfilled splendidly, was to introduce in a scientific and coherent manner the idea that below the superbly "civilized" surface of the cultured European man was a "subconscious" realm entranced in chaos. Satisfying the exacting criteria of academicians and scientists, he demonstrated that human beings, as well as entire cultures, are composed of collections of subconscious drives, compulsions, and conflicts. He convinced prudish Victorians that sex and sexuality were of great importance to the well-being of men and women, and he revealed the implications of repression and frustration of the libido. This was Freud's karmic mission, his link in the chain of evolving human understanding. To fulfill this function he needed to be born at a time and place (and within certain environmental conditions) that afforded him the determination and will power, as well as the intelligence and understanding, necessary to innovate and promote these concepts. It was, similarly, the mission of Jung and others to expand upon and make certain adjustments to the mainstream of psychoanalytic thought and practice.

One further point of significance is the remarkable zodiacal phase arc of 51°23' between Freud's moon and its north lunar node. This distance is only three minutes of an arc from an exact septile aspect. The contact suggests that Freud's individuality had just crossed the threshold to a new realm of energy utilization, enabling him to probe into previously unknown and irrational realms of human existence as well as entitling him to carry the responsibility of presenting to humanity a new image of man.

C. G. JUNG: A NATAL PERSPECTIVE

Carl Gustav Jung was born in Kesswill, Switzerland, on July 26, 1875, at 7:20 P.M. The pattern of his chart is striking: The planets are distributed in a gestalt that closely approaches a five-pointed star. Five-, six-, and seven-pointed star patterns are probably the most challenging of all patterns to decipher, not only because of their rarity but also because very few of our consciousnesses are yet attuned to the level of being they represent. A five-pointed star pattern might tentatively be interpreted as signifying an individualistic temperament with potentially pronounced creative, synthesizing capabilities.

Jung was at the forefront of Freud's psychoanalytic movement and was regarded as Freud's heir apparent for many years—until the two eventually ended their association because of some ideological differences. When their charts are compared, Freud and Jung appear to be working with similar zodiacal energies with emphasis on the Taurus-Scorpio and Leo-Aquarius axes. Along house-oriented lines as well, both have an emphasis around the descendant, and Mars in the eleventh house. Distinctions emerge when we consider Jung's soli-lunar type and the pattern made by the aspects between his planets.

Jung is a third-quarter moon type, having a 282°09' phase arc between the sun and moon. This soli-lunar type symbolizes a future-oriented individual, one who strives for the understanding and application of universal principles. Rudhyar writes in *The Lunation Cycle* that the third-quarter type is essentially characterized by a tendency to experience crisis in *consciousness*; at least what seems mainly important to these persons is the embodiment of their ideological beliefs in definite systems of thought and/or concrete institutions. [p. 54]

The mid-Taurus moon and early Leo sun, in the third and seventh houses, add determination and individualistic qualities to Jung's third-quarter moon type that might have been most easily channeled through his experiences of relating with the environment (physical, emotional, and mental) and his interchange with others. The Sabian symbols for the zodiacal and house-oriented positions of Jung's natal sun reveal a great complexity in his solar purpose. The symbol for Jung's zodiacal sun (124 or the fourth degree of Leo) reads, "*A formally dressed elderly man stands near trophies he brought back from a hunting expedition.*" Rudhyar describes this symbol in *An Astrological Mandala* as, "the masculine will to conquer his animal nature and to impress his peers with his skill in performing the ancient traditional power rituals." The symbol for this degree sheds some light on Jung's claim to be an introvert (though astrologers have often referred to him as an outgoing Leo) while, according to his fundamental typology, he classified Freud as predominantly an extrovert. Jung probably meant that he was more concerned than was Freud with channeling his solar energy toward his own internal, spiritual growth than with establishing himself as an authority or in a position of external power. The Sabian symbol for Jung's sun speaks of the drive toward self-perfection, and as it also implies, Jung was not without his own brand of leonine pride.

Moving from the level of *vital energy* (zodiacal sun) to the sphere of *experiential purpose* (house-oriented sun), we find an interesting contrast between the two frames of reference when considering the Sabian symbol for Jung's house-oriented sun. The symbol for this degree (phase 185) is: "*A man revealing to his students the foundation of an inner knowledge upon which a 'new world' could be built.*" This symbolic statement sums up Jung's role in revealing to modern humanity a spiritual approach to the understanding and evolution of human consciousness.

The aspects in Jung's chart compose two major formations, as

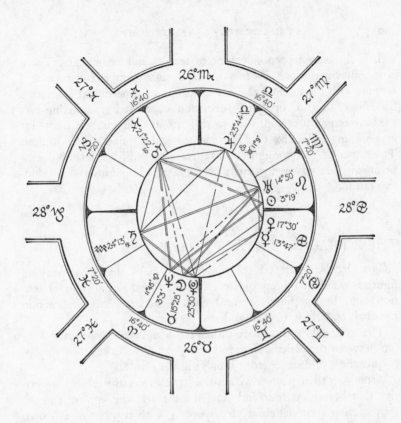

C. G. Jung's Birth Chart

	☉ 123°19'	☽ 45°28'	☿ 103°47'	♀ 107°30'	♂ 261°22'	♃ 203°44'	♄ 324°13'	♅ 134°50'	♆ 33°3'	♇ 53°30
☉ 184:3		283	341	345	222	280	160	349	91	70
☽ 81:58	258		302	298	145	202	82	271	13	352
☿ 159:22	336	283		357	203	261	140	329	71	51
♀ 164:45	345	278	355		207	264	144	333	75	54
♂ 306:50	238	136	213	218		58	298	127	229	208
♃ 245:24	299	197	274	280	62		240	69	171	151
♄ 19:53	165	63	140	145	287	226		190	292	271
♅ 192:49	352	250	327	332	114	53	188		102	82
♆ 72:30	112	10	87	93	235	173	308	121		340
♇ 88:5	96	354	72	77	219	158	292	105	345	

well as showing a preponderance of sextiles and quincunxes. There is a somewhat loose T-cross in fixed signs between Saturn and Uranus with the moon and Pluto at its apex. Of particular interest is the "finger of god" or "yod" formation, composed of a waxing sextile between Jupiter and Mars, with Pluto at their indirect midpoint in a waning quincunx to Mars and a waxing quincunx to Jupiter. The finger-of-god configuration represents a sensitive, intuitive temperament that strives to clarify issues in a harmonious and productive fashion.

THE ZODIACAL CONTACT CHART

The circular chart on the upper portion of the accompanying figure is the Freud-Jung zodiacal contact chart. Freud's (inner section) and Jung's (outer section) natal planets are arranged within the chart according to their zodiacal positions.

The grid below the chart displays the zodiacal phase arcs existing between the planets of Freud and Jung. Freud's sun (46°21′) is, for instance, 77 degrees from Jung's sun (123°19′).

Arranging their planets within the structure of the zodiac we notice that Freud has four and Jung has three in the sign of Taurus, representing a mutual ability for working with energies of a "down to earth," practical type, and a common capacity for endurance and determination. One of the most significant contacts between the two charts is a close conjunction between Freud's natal sun at 16°21′ Taurus and Jung's moon at 15°28′ Taurus—signifying that the two men were able to tap the same energy source. The fifteenth degree of Taurus—the midpoint of the first quarter of the zodiac—represents the point of release for the dynamic energy directed toward the formation of a self-conscious personality. It is, therefore, a powerful symbol of unity for these two men who have done so much to advance our understanding of the human personality. The energy combination of an active solar principle (Freud's sun) and a receptive, intuitive lunar principle (Jung's moon) probably inspired the personalities and lives of the two much more deeply than has been commonly recognized. Indeed, Freud represents the masculine element of the relationship with Jung; while Jung, after leav-

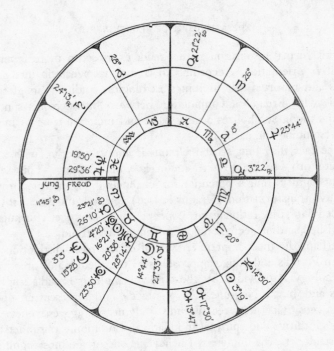

Freud-Jung Zodiacal Contact Chart

	☉ 46°21'	☽ 74°44'	☿ 58°14'	♀ 26°10'	♂ 183°22'	♃ 359°36'	♄ 87°33'	♅ 50°38'	♆ 349°50'	♇ 34°20'
☉ 123°19'	77	49	66	98	300	124	36	73	134	89
☽ 45°28'	360	331	348	20	223	46	318	355	56	12
☿ 103°47'	58	30	46	78	281	105	17	54	114	70
♀ 107°30'	62	33	50	82	285	108	20	57	118	74
♂ 261°22'	216	187	204	236	78	262	174	211	272	228
♃ 203°44'	158	129	146	178	21	205	117	154	214	170
♄ 324°13'	278	250	266	299	141	325	237	274	335	290
♅ 134°50'	89	61	77	109	312	136	48	85	145	101
♆ 33°3'	347	319	335	7	210	34	306	343	44	359
♇ 53°30'	8	339	356	28	231	54	326	3	64	20

ing his formal association with Freud, expressed a more feminine, intuitive orientation. According to traditional synastric interpretations and reported also in Jung's astrological studies years after his break with Freud,[1] a conjunction between one person's sun and other's moon symbolizes a very basic and inclusive type of mutual understanding and harmony.

The fact that Jung's natal Uranus is almost exactly (with a six-minute orb) sextile Freud's moon is worth noting. This sextile might signify Jung's potential for channeling his energies toward creative transformation (Uranus in Leo) and to some extent toward challenging the rationalized concepts and practices formulated, nourished, and protected (moon in Gemini) by Freud.

Perhaps the most impressive symbol of the basic distinctions between Freud's and Jung's approaches to the theory and practice of psychology is provided by the quincunx linking Freud's singleton Mars and Jung's Neptune. This contact could represent an underlying sensitivity between Freud's judgmental aggressiveness and Jung's intuitive and spiritual foundations. Commonly misunderstood by astrologers, the quincunx, I believe, is one of the most significant aspects in synastry. It operates powerfully on a level of relationship that most of us find confusing: the reorientation of the way in which one uses his or her personal energies. It calls for a choice between a largely unconscious, compulsive use of personal energies or their conscious, purposeful expression. When we meet and work closely with a person who has a planet or angle forming a close quincunx with one of our natal factors, these alternatives should be kept in mind. Individuals are often mysteriously drawn to one another by a quincunx; for instance, often experiencing alternating feelings of love and hate, attraction and repulsion. In the instance of Freud and Jung, the Mars-Neptune quincunx brought to the surface of their relationship not only what they had in common (and that was a great deal) but also the feelings, experiences, and energies they did not share. Apparently, after a time, the repulsive energies outweighed the attractive, especially from Jung's point of view. The break between Freud and Jung, of course, was inevitable; a part, as we shall discuss in greater detail later, of the natural unfoldment of a process. Through the experiences he gained from his close association with the master of psychoanalysis, Jung was able to focus on his own ideas more clearly and come to the decision (quincunx) that their great differences demanded a separation of energies (the opposition phase of any cycle of relationship), since it was apparent, at least to Jung, that he could no longer work with Freud in a harmonious manner (the trine phase of unfoldment).

There is another quincunx, between Jung's Mars and Freud's Uranus. This quincunx, however, could be interpreted as manifesting its potentiality in a manner directed toward harmonious adjustment. Jung recognized Freud throughout as the great originator of psychoanalysis and as a man whose innovative concepts and revolutionary ideas (Uranus) had greatly promoted Jung's own understanding of psychology. He consistently defended (Mars stationary) Freud during the time when Freud was virtually *persona non grata* in academic and professional circles. Jung's initial decision to commit himself to Freud's work took a great deal of courage and conviction.

THE HOUSE CONTACT CHART

The Freud-Jung house contact chart is illustrated in the accompanying figure. It, and the phase grid below it, are organized in the same manner as the zodiacal contact chart, except that it is derived from the house-oriented positions of Freud's and Jung's natal planets rather than their zodiacal orientations.

The house contact chart of Freud and Jung reveals several interesting points. Jung's chart, with five planets on each side of the meridian, tends to balance Freud's predominantly Western hemispheric chart (nine planets to the right of the meridian): Through Freud's relationship with Jung, his (Freud's) concepts had a channel for reconciling self with other. What their relationship ultimately produced (through Jung) was an approach to the nature of the human psyche that transcended the view of man as a collection of drives, urges, and impulses molded by his environment. (This was Freud's view and is an expression of a Western hemispheric preponderance.) Through Jung, however, an image of man was eventually introduced as possessing an inherent order and purpose on both individual and collective levels.

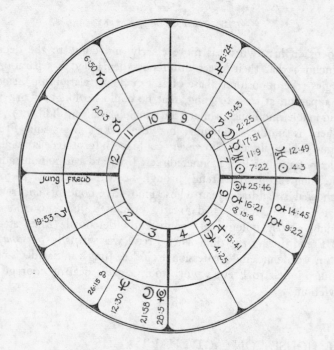

Freud-Jung House Contact Chart

	☉ 187:22	☽ 212:25	☿ 197:51	♀ 166:21	♂ 320:3	♃ 135:41	♄ 223:43	♅ 191:9	♆ 124:25	♇ 175:46
☉ 184:3	357	332	347	18	225	49	321	353	60	9
☽ 81:58	255	230	245	276	122	307	219	251	318	267
☿ 159:22	332	307	322	354	200	24	296	329	35	344
♀ 164:45	338	313	327	359	205	30	302	334	41	349
♂ 306:50	120	95	109	141	347	172	84	116	183	132
♃ 245:24	59	33	48	80	286	110	22	55	121	70
♄ 19:53	193	168	183	214	60	245	157	189	256	205
♅ 192:49	6	341	355	27	233	58	330	2	69	18
♆ 72:30	246	221	235	267	113	297	209	242	309	257
♇ 88:5	261	236	251	282	129	313	225	257	324	273

The sixth house (personal conflicts and reorientation, as well as the psychoanalytic process) is particularly significant in the charts of both Freud and Jung. Freud has Pluto, Venus, and the north lunar node, and Jung has Venus and Mercury in this house. There is a close contact between Freud's north lunar node (occupying the fourteenth section of the sixth house) and Jung's Venus (at the fifteenth section of his sixth house). This points to a potentially sensitive and evolutionary (north lunar node) mental (Mercury) relationship between the two men. Since the mutual field of experience through which this potentiality can best develop is represented by the sixth house, this process should involve a good deal of work and a transformation of both personalities. A transformation apparently did occur as their relationship grew, but in spite of their mutual respect and affection (both have Venus in nearly the same section of the sixth house) a completely positive reorientation of the two personalities and an integration of their life work was too much for them to actualize, and in 1922 they formally ended their association of fifteen years. This does not mean, of course, that their relationship entirely ceased to exist—relatedness transcends physical or direct contact.

A look at some significant contacts occurring in the seventh house of formal relationship and partnership provides additional insight into Freud's and Jung's association. The seventh house of Freud's chart contains the sun, Uranus, and Mercury; Jung's natal seventh house contains the sun and Uranus. Another contact exists between Freud's Uranus and Jung's sun. This points to the potentiality of a relationship of the most dynamic, innovative, and possibly disruptive type—and is another symbol of the potential for transformation in the lives of the two individuals, affecting their concepts of self and relatedness in the deepest sense. Other significant factors in the contact chart include a house-oriented opposition between Freud's Neptune and Jung's Mars and a square between Freud's Venus and Jung's Neptune.

HOUSE TRANSPOSITION CHARTS

The house contact chart is a map describing mutual fields of experience. House transposition charts constructed by placing the natal planets of one person into the house structure of another, complement house contact charts by helping the astrologer to come to an understanding of how one person experiences the other.

By placing Jung's natal planets into Freud's house structure we can get an idea of how Freud experienced Jung: what areas of

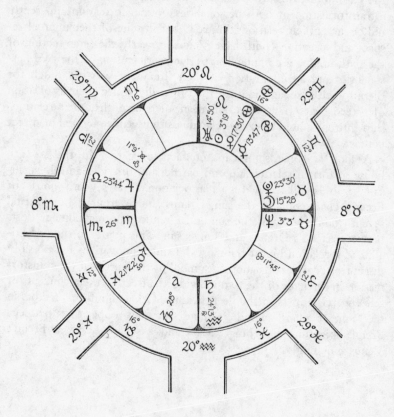

Freud's Houses—Jung's Planets

Freud's experience were stimulated by him. A few of the more significant features of this chart include Freud's second house occupied by Jung's Mars, stationary direct, in the twenty-second degree of Sagittarius, a possible symbol of Freud's possessive attitude toward Jung's ideas and concepts. Jung's ascendant falls in Freud's natal third house, promoting concrete mental activities. Jung might have been responsible for bringing out some of Freud's inner feelings of personal inadequacy and insecurity; his Saturn is located in Freud's fourth house, just past the I.C. The ninth house is particularly emphasized in this chart as well, with Jung's Venus, sun, and Uranus therein—stimulating and possibly even disrupting Freud's

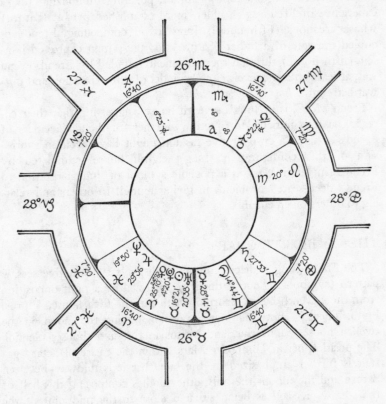

Jung's Houses—Freud's Planets

abstract and philosophical outlook. Jung's Neptune, moon, and Pluto surrounding Freud's descendant is representative of Freud's experience of Jung as someone with whom he could relate closely in both abstract and mundane activities.

In Jung's experience we find Freud's condensed group of nine planets in Jung's second, third, fourth, and fifth houses—symbolizing experiences of having, knowing, self-integration, and self-expression. Jung's contact with Freud was a greatly stimulating influence on Jung's mental development—represented here by four of Freud's planets (Venus, Pluto, sun, and Uranus) falling into Jung's third house. Freud's natal Saturn falls exactly on the halfway point (midpoint) of Jung's second quadrant, possibly symbolizing Jung's experience of Freud as an older, more established person (Saturn) whose creations (fifth house) Jung found compelling. Freud occupied the role of a father (Saturn) to Jung; Jung expressed himself (fifth house) through the movement founded by Freud. Freud was, at least on some levels, Jung's model of self-expression and outward strength.

Freud's M.C. is in Jung's seventh house, suggesting that their capacity, at least initially, to function together for the achievement of Freud's goals in a co-operative fashion might have been an expression of this configuration. Jung's eighth house, stimulated by Freud's singleton Mars, is a possible symbol of Jung's reaction to Freud's deep-seated problems in giving himself to others and relating to others on an equal basis.

THE COMPOSITE CHART

The Freud-Jung zodiacal composite displays a distinctive seesaw pattern (symbolizing active duality) polarized by a tight opposition from the eleventh house, Scorpio, Mars and the fifth house, Taurus, Pluto. There is another looser opposition linking the moon, in the twelfth house, Sagittarius, and Venus in the sixth house, Gemini. The position of the composite Mars within the entire planetary gestalt is further emphasized by the fact that it is midway between Saturn and the moon—the only other bodies composing this half of the seesaw—as well as being situated close to the midpoint of the fourth quadrant.

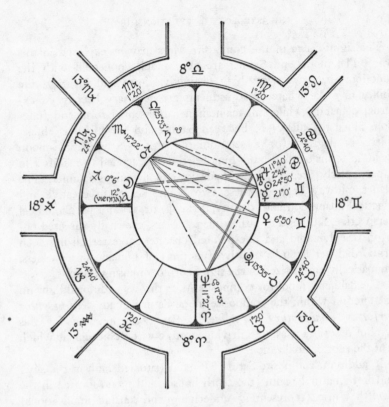

Freud-Jung Composite Chart

	☉ 84°50'	☽ 240°6'	☿ 81°1'	♀ 66°50'	♂ 222°22'	♃ 101°40'	♄ 205°53'	♅ 92°44'	♆ 11°27'	♇ 43°55'
☉ 185:35		156	357	342	223	344	239	353	74	41
☽ 338:3	153		160	174	18	139	35	148	229	197
☿ 182:28	357	156		15	219	340	236	349	70	38
♀ 168:1	343	171	15		205	326	221	335	56	23
♂ 316:20	230	22	227	212		121	17	130	211	179
♃ 199:25	347	139	344	329	117		256	9	91	58
♄ 296:28	250	42	246	232	20	263		114	195	162
♅ 192:5	354	146	351	336	125	8	105		82	49
♆ 95:5	91	243	88	73	222	105	202	97		328
♇ 138:37	47	200	44	30	178	61	158	54	317	

The significance of the composite Mars may be explored in this way: The moon and Saturn are very much connected with the functions that give everything distinctive form and identity; the ability to make whatever adjustments are necessary because of external demands, while still maintaining an essential form and function. Since the phase arc between Saturn and the moon is almost thirty-six degrees (or a semi-quintile aspect), the Saturn-moon dyad, in terms of the Freud-Jung relationship, tended to manifest in a particularly creative, individualistic, and ingenious manner. The planet midway between these two bodies serves in creative and practical adaptation and identity forming, or, from a psychological perspective, mother and father images. Mars, externally directed energy, is a dynamic and one-pointed channel for externalizing such primordial yet latently creative functions of human consciousness, dramatically emphasized in the sign Scorpio, opposing Pluto.

The Sabian symbol for composite Mars throws additional light on its function within the composite moon-Saturn dyad: *"An inventor performs a laboratory experiment."* Rudhyar's keynote for this symbol describes it as "the driving urge toward achievement which is at the root of civilization."

In addition, composite Saturn elevated (situated high in the sky) and in its natural realm (the tenth house) and moon located in the twelfth house (representing underlying and karmic implications) correspond with the psychological distinctions between the rational, masculine (Saturn in the tenth) and the irrational, intuitive (moon in the twelfth) modes of consciousness that play significant roles in the psychologies of both Freud and Jung. The axis of the conscious/unconscious and all it implies is also stressed by the Mars-Pluto opposition.

Freud's natal Mars falls close to the composite M.C., suggesting both his desire to maintain a superior position with Jung at all times and Jung's experience of Freud as a father figure. Jung's Mars opposite composite Mercury and natal Mercury on composite Jupiter symbolize the vast potential their relationship held for Jung (and for Freud via Jung) in terms of mental stimulation and expansion of philosophical horizons. Jung's natal Jupiter on composite Saturn is an apt symbol for his ability to be closely associated with Freud without becoming completely overwhelmed by Freud's influence.

GEORGE SAND AND FREDERIC CHOPIN

GEORGE SAND: A NATAL PERSPECTIVE

George Sand, the feminist novelist, was born Aurore Lucile Dupin in Paris on July 1, 1804, at 10:15 P.M.

Her birth chart has an open-angle planetary pattern, with overtones of a seesaw pattern. All of her planets are more or less evenly distributed within 240 degrees, with only one house vacant within the occupied area. The empty fifth house, however, tends to set the planets apart into two loosely defined groups, giving the chart a hint of duality characterizing the seesaw pattern that has all ten planets divided into two distinct, opposing groups. The open-angle pattern denotes a personality that is open to the diversity of life and the transcendent element of experience. The entire planetary gestalt is held together by Pluto in the first house, Pisces, and Neptune in the ninth house, Scorpio. The phase arc of these two planets is 253°36′ zodiacally; 240°36′ (a very close trine) from a house orientation. The fact that all other planetary bodies fall within the span of the Pluto-Neptune phase arc gives added significance to the transcendental implications of the open-angle pattern; the essentializing (Pluto) and universalizing (Neptune) functions of these two planets permeate and structure the entire planetary makeup of the chart.

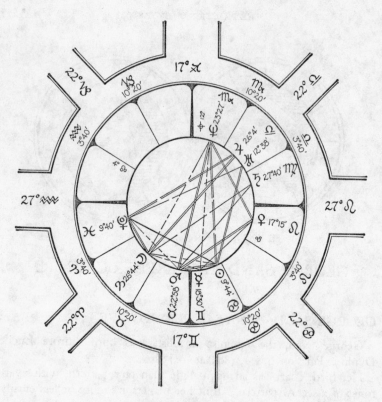

George Sand's Birth Chart

	☉ 99°44'	☽ 26°44'	☿ 78°30'	♀ 137°15'	♂ 52°58'	♃ 206°4'	♄ 177°40'	♅ 192°38'	♆ 233°27'	♇ 339°40'
☉ 109:15		287	339	38	47	254	283	268	227	121
☽ 48:51	290		309	250	334	181	210	195	154	48
☿ 91:56	333	317		302	26	233	261	246	206	99
♀ 167:29	49	242	285		85	292	320	305	264	158
♂ 70:21	49	339	22	98		207	236	221	180	74
♃ 228:20	251	181	224	300	203		29	14	333	227
♄ 205:6	275	204	247	323	226	24		346	305	198
♅ 217:21	262	192	235	311	214	11	348		320	213
♆ 250:50	229	159	202	277	180	338	315	327		254
♇ 10:22	109	39	82	158	60	218	195	207	241	

The midpoint axis of the significant Pluto-Neptune phase arc can serve as an indicator of the focus of George Sand's pattern of self and more specifically reveal how the transcendental, reformulative functions of the Pluto-Neptune pair could have been integrated within her entire being. This axis extends, zodiacally, from the seventeenth degree of Cancer to the seventeenth degree of Capricorn, close to the second and fourth quadrant midpoints—emphasizing the experiences of self and social expression. The direct midpoint, denoting the conscious, externalizing pole of the axis, is in the otherwise unoccupied fifth house of creativity and self-expression. This suggests that Sand could consciously center and integrate herself through fifth house experiences. The mode of energy that projected her through these experiences is characterized by the maternalistic sign of Cancer. The Sabian symbol for the midpoint (seventeen Cancer) expresses the vastness and complexity of her creative, self-expressing energies: *"The unfoldment of multilevel potentialities issuing from an original germ."* George Sand was not only a woman of extraordinary creative potential—manifested through the hundred or more books that flowed from her pen— but also a great inspiration to all those who knew her and read her novels. The indirect pole of this axis, situated at seventeen Capricorn in the eleventh house of social expression and participation, denotes the type of experiences and energy that Sand was striving to integrate into her pattern of being.

The direct midpoint symbolizes where Sand was coming from (her Pluto-Neptune pair being representative of her basic orientation toward multifunctional life). Conversely, the indirect midpoint represents where her life should lead her, particularly by way of the many transcendental, regenerative experiences that encouraged her to identify with the unconventional, transformative movements of her time—characterized by the position of this point in her eleventh house as well as by her strong Aquarius-Leo horizon. The Sabian symbol for the indirect midpoint suggests Sand's need to go beyond the role her culture usually assigned women; it reads, *"A repressed woman finds psychological release in nudism."* Rudhyar's keynote remarks that this symbol portrays "the escape from bondage to social inhibitions and a reliance upon the wisdom of the body."

Although George Sand was married to Casmir Dudevant while

still in her teens and had a son by him in 1823, she soon rebelled against the traditional role of wife and mother. In 1831, at the age of twenty-six, she left her country home for Paris. According to the one-degree system of direction, her natal Mars progressed to a conjunction with natal Mercury, her moon progressed to a conjunction with natal Mars, and her Jupiter reached a conjunction with natal Neptune at that time. During the following year her first novel, *Indiana*, was published under the pseudonym "George Sand," which eventually became her adopted name. A sketch of the trials of her married life and her eventual liberation, it was an immediate success. Many other novels followed, all explications of the main theme of her life—the power of love to renew the soul and transcend the obstacles of social conventions and morality. They portrayed women's struggle for the rights of self-expression and self-determination in a male-dominated world. The contents of her literary works, along with her eccentric, bold, and free-loving life style, distinguish her as one of the initiating forces of the feminist movement.

George Sand, like Carl Jung, is a third-quarter soli-lunar type (there is a 287° phase arc between sun and moon) suggesting an inclination toward the pursuit of new ideals and the potential for understanding abstract, universal life principles. The phase arc between the dynamic and productive Aries, second house moon and the self-integrating Cancer sun in the fourth house is that of a waning/applying quintile with a one-degree orb. This configuration could signify Sand's ability for creatively releasing her new ideals to a wide public in a technically effective and innovative way that not only provided for her immediate mundane needs (moon in the second) but also gave vital, personal meaning to her existence (Cancer sun in the fourth house).

The sun also forms an applying/waning square with Uranus in the eighth house, Libra, symbolic of a drive toward experiencing intense and individual, as well as artistic and sensitive, interpersonal relationships as a mean of self-transformation. A dynamic separating/waning tri-octile links the sun with the focal Neptune—emphasizing Sand's already intense sensual, transcendental (Neptune in Scorpio) and philosophical (ninth house) inclinations and opening for her a channel for the wide dissemination of her ideals. Neptune (the symbol of the universal and transcendental love that Sand so often tried to personalize in her novels and in the course of her own life) is situated in the ninth house of publication and connected with the mental planet Mercury (in the communicative sign of Gemini, located near her natal I.C.) by a very close applying/waning tri-septile aspect. This link-up suggests that George Sand had the potential to perform a very special social, cultural function through effectively communicating, in the most direct and personal terms (Mercury in Gemini on the I.C.), the need to reorient antiquated ideals concerning the essential value of the romantic, individual element of life with the need for a transpersonal view of life in general (Neptune in ninth house, Scorpio).

The Sabian symbol for the position of Mercury speaks of this process (from its mental, Mercurial perspective): *"A large volume reveals traditional wisdom."* Rudhyar's keynote for the symbol is, "contacting the all-human planetary Mind underlying any cultural and personal mentality." The Sabian symbol for the zodiacal position of Neptune complements Mercury's function in this process and suggests that Sand closely identified herself with her transcendental function as an inspirer and transformer of cultural values. It reads: *"After having heard an inspired individual deliver his 'sermon on the Mount,' crowds are returning home."* The keynote for his symbol describes "the need to incorporate inspiring experiences and teachings into everyday living."

The meaning I suggest for the general planetary situation described above is further supported and brought into a powerfully personal and immediate focus by the fact that Neptune forms a very tight applying opposition with Mars in the fourth house, Taurus, and both are in turn connected by constructive, confrontative squares to her sixth house Venus in Leo. This configuration is an apt symbol for Sand's artistic and philosophical prolificity as well as her sensitivity toward the struggles of the repressed.

FREDERIC CHOPIN: A NATAL PERSPECTIVE

The renowned pianist-composer, Frederic Chopin, was born at Zelazowa, Wola, near Warsaw, Poland, on March 1, 1810, at 6:00 P.M. His father, Nicholas Chopin, was born in France but immigrated to Poland in his youth, never returning to his native land and becoming completely identified with the Polish culture. His family was not of the higher, ruling class, but Nicholas was a tutor engaged by aristocratic families, and young Frederic was brought up in refined, sophisticated surroundings. Chopin became a natural aristocrat and was able to fit in comfortably when his extraordinary talents had introduced him to upper-class society while he was still a youth.

It was not until Chopin had traveled to Paris, however, at that time the hub of European culture and the vital center of the romantic movement, that he found creative elements with which he could identify. In spite of the fact that he spent the rest of his life away from Poland, however, Chopin considered himself Polish and preferred the company of Polish aristocrats. His exceptional talents as a sensitive and innovative pianist and composer were recognized in 1836 by the same Parisian artistic circles in which George Sand had established herself as a most dynamic, controversial woman. Shortly after his arrival in Paris, Chopin was introduced to the trouser-wearing, cigar-smoking Sand by her intimate friend, Franz Lizst. During the following year, in spite of Chopin's great reluctance due to an emotional attachment to another woman in his past and his rather conventional Catholic views on sexuality, they engaged in "a poem," as Chopin liked to call their affair, that endured for more than eight years.

Chopin's birth chart exhibits a hemispheric planetary pattern, defined by Jupiter and the moon, containing all eight other planetary bodies within the span of a loose opposition aspect. The hemispheric pattern presents duality in its most distinct form—the interplay between actuality and potentiality; the apparent and the underlying; the conscious and unconscious—by having all planets within one half of the circle of the chart. In terms of personal psychology it represents a person faced with the challenge to integrate both poles of life within his or her personality.

The chart's center of gravity, the midpoint axis of the Jupiter-moon pair, symbolizes the basic focus for this challenge of integration. This axis extends from eighteen Cancer (the cyclic midpoint of the Jupiter-moon pair) to eighteen Capricorn (the indirect midpoint and the center of gravity for the occupied hemisphere), only

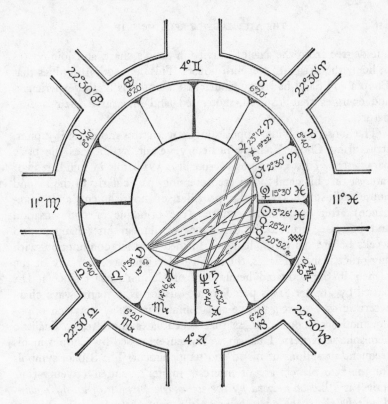

Frederic Chopin's Birth Chart

	☉ 333°26'	☽ 191°58'	☿ 320°52'	♀ 328°21'	♂ 2°30	♃ 23°12	♄ 254°32'	♅ 224°15'	♆ 248°40'	♇ 345°30'
☉ 172:59		213	13	355	331	311	79	110	85	348
☽ 33:34	221		232	224	190	169	298	328	304	207
☿ 161:19	12	233		8	319	298	67	97	73	336
♀ 168:15	356	226	7		326	306	74	105	80	343
♂ 203:19	330	191	319	325		340	108	139	114	17
♃ 225:45	308	168	296	303	338		129	159	135	38
♄ 99:46	74	294	62	69	104	126		31	6	270
♅ 68:35	105	325	93	100	135	158	32		336	239
♆ 94:20	79	300	67	74	109	132	6	335		264
♇ 184:53	349	209	337	344	19	41	275	244	270	

one degree from the axis of gravity in Sand's chart, and joining (as in hers) the fifth and eleventh houses. This connection signifies that Chopin and Sand had very similar paths in terms of the experiences and energies that inspired, motivated, and integrated their overall natures.

The loose, applying opposition between the moon and Jupiter, structuring Chopin's entire planetary gestalt, symbolizes the basic parameters of his conscious personality. With this in mind, it is of interest that his natal moon (representing, particularly in the second house, adjustments and the provider of nourishment and sustenance) after conjuncting Jupiter (the principle of compensation and increase, situated in the house of human interchange) two weeks before his birth, had not formed another conjunction with any other planet. That is, the moon had yet to pass over any of the planets in the activated hemisphere of Chopin's chart since it last passed by Jupiter. This paradoxical situation is in many ways characteristic of a most sensitive and complex interplay between opposite modes of consciousness that accentuates the already dualistic hemispheric pattern. Dualism was often expressed by Chopin in his frequent alterations of mood and temperament. The Sabian symbols for the two planets are of interest. Jupiter's symbol (twenty-four Aries) is: "*Blown inward by the wind, the curtains of an open window take the shape of a cornucopia*"; with a keynote that mentions "openness to the influx of spiritual energies." The symbol for the moon's position speaks directly to the fact that the lunar function is about to emerge from the depths of the unconscious to a conscious realm of multifunctional activity: "*Miners are surfacing from a deep coal mine.*"

Chopin was born about two and a half days after the full moon, indicating a life purpose geared toward contact with others with fulfillment and success to come through an essential receptivity to whatever experiences come one's way. In *The Lunation Cycle* Rudhyar explains that in the full-moon type

objectivity and clear consciousness as the result of interpersonal and social-cultural relationships are, theoretically, the basic factors in character . . . What was mainly *felt* in the past is now *seen*. This may mean a revelation or illumination, and normally some kind of fulfillment; but it can also mean, negatively, separation or divorce—perhaps even a divorce from reality, or inner division ("man against himself"). [pp. 52–53]

Whereas George Sand's sun and moon are linked by a waning quintile, Chopin's soli-lunar pair have just passed the waning biquintile. This would indicate the creative and artistic compatibility between the two that afforded not only mutual inspiration but also a capacity for Sand and Chopin to share immediate, mundane life experiences through cohabitation (both have moon in the second house) in a way that brought out the best of both of them. However, Chopin was not an easy man to get along with, either superficially or intimately: His conservative, emotionally sensitive and withdrawn nature, signified by Pisces sun and the inner planets (Mercury and Venus) in the sixth house as well as by the Virgo-Pisces horizon, manifested itself through almost constant inner turmoil and difficulty in accepting others.

THE ZODIACAL CONTACT CHART

The Sand-Chopin zodiacal contact chart reveals many significant and powerful connections existing between the two in terms of the interplay of multifunctional energies.

Perhaps the most revealing of these contacts are the tri-octiles that link both Sand's ascendant with Chopin's moon, and Sand's moon with Chopin's ascendant. These configurations denote again that Sand and Chopin found one another mutually stimulating and encouraging in terms of day-to-day life experiences (moon) and had the potential to use this stimulation as a means of realizing their innermost purposes and selves (ascendant). Sand's Uranus is less than one degree from Chopin's moon: strengthening the intensity of the moon-ascendant tri-octiles, as well as adding to it the elements of upheaval and the unexpected. Chopin's zodiacal Venus is very close to Sand's ascendant, contributing an element of identification and mutual appreciation of each other's artistic, aesthetic sensitivities.

The waxing/separating tri-septiles linking Sand's Cancer sun with

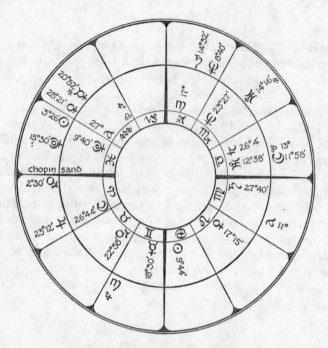

Sand-Chopin Zodiacal Contact Chart

	☉ 99°44'	☽ 26°41'	☿ 78°30'	♀ 137°15'	♂ 52°58'	♃ 206°4'	♄ 177°40'	♅ 192°38'	♆ 233°27'	♇ 339°40'
☉ 333°26'	234	307	255	197	281	128	156	141	100	354
☽ 191°58'	93	166	114	55	139	346	15	360	319	213
☿ 320°52'	222	295	243	184	268	115	144	129	88	342
♀ 328°21'	229	302	250	192	276	123	151	136	95	349
♂ 2°30'	263	336	284	226	310	157	185	170	130	23
♃ 23°12'	284	357	305	246	331	178	206	191	150	44
♄ 254°32'	155	228	177	118	202	49	77	62	22	275
♅ 224°16'	125	198	146	88	172	19	47	32	351	245
♆ 248°40'	149	222	171	112	196	43	71	57	16	269
♇ 345°30'	246	319	267	209	293	140	168	153	113	6

Chopin's Sagittarius Saturn and Sand's late Virgo Saturn with Chopin's Pisces sun, constitute a most unusual connection for the integration of one's basic center of self and purpose with the other's personal limitations and mundane identity. This contact could also signify karmic factors that may have brought the two together for the fulfillment of a transpersonal purpose. The fact that Chopin's Saturn is situated close to Sand's natal M.C. indicates that Sand and Chopin were able to do much to further one another's position in the outer world as well. Chopin's fourth house Saturn on Sand's M.C. could, in addition, reflect that through the eight years that the two lived together, Sand was the one who largely managed and provided for nearly all their domestic and financial needs. George Sand's Mercury is, however, opposed to Chopin's Saturn. Even though their Mercurys are trine—symbolic of easy, harmonious communication at least on the mental, verbal level—Sand and Chopin often did not agree. The Mercury-Saturn opposition could be interpreted as Sand's inability to accept Chopin's class prejudices and his adherence to many outmoded social conventions.

The tight tri-octile between Sand's Venus and Chopin's Mars signifies an exciting, intense, but often conflicting and confrontative, emotional/sexual relationship, given additional impetus by the square between Sand's Venus and Chopin's Uranus and as well as by Chopin's Venus forming tri-octile with Sand's Uranus. We know very little about their emotional and sexual life together, except that they were both immediately and compulsively drawn toward one another (in Chopin's instance the attraction was so strong that he initially tried his best to avoid Sand), a situation quite likely to be an experience of the strong Uranus-Venus aspects.

There are, of course, many other relevant zodiacal contacts between these two charts, but it is not my intention to present a lengthy catalogue of such configurations here. Sand and Chopin had a most complex relationship that was in many ways paradoxical. Whereas George Sand was one of the most revolutionary, outrageous individuals of her time, especially in her flaunting of social restraints and conventions, Chopin worshipped social order and was himself a most aristocratic man. Sand had one of the true transcendental minds of her time, guided by an inner sense of morality, regarding sex as a deeply spiritual act. Chopin was a devout Catholic, a social prude, and, at least before his liaison with Sand, had an abhorrence for sex—attitudes that offended Sand's more liberated views. In a letter composed during the early months of their friendship, Sand writes to a mutual friend of theirs concerning Chopin's attitude that "certain acts" might ruin everything.

> I have always been repelled by this [Chopin's] attitude toward the ultimate embrace of love. If it is not as sacred, as pure, as consecrated an act as the rest, there is no virtue in abstaining. The word *physical* which people use to describe something which has no name except in the higher region, displeases and *shocks* me . . . [as quoted in Frances Winwar's *George Sand and Her Times;* p. 320]

These two creative individuals, in spite of their differences, were able to come together, however, in a basically harmonious manner. In a very real way they assisted each other along their individual paths of fulfillment, in turn contributing greatly to the whole of humanity. Perhaps it is because there were so many contradictory and mysterious elements involved in their relationship that Chopin's biographers usually describe George Sand as a devouring female who ruined Chopin and was probably the cause of his early death. While it is true that Sand was a very strong woman (this in itself was probably enough to set most journalists against her), such views are far from accurate. Chopin's work excelled during his contact with Sand. She supported him materially (his compositions were, during his lifetime, still too innovative to receive wide support and he almost never gave public concerts) and took care of him physically. Chopin died of tuberculosis at the age of thirty-nine, shortly after his break with Sand.

THE HOUSE CONTACT CHART

From a house-oriented perspective, the charts of Sand and Chopin are quite similar. Both have all planets within the first, second, and third quadrants, and within these quadrants both have

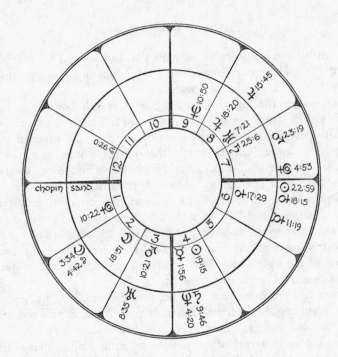

Sand-Chopin House Contact Chart

	☉ 109:15	☽ 48:51	☿ 91:56	♀ 167:29	♂ 70:21	♃ 228:20	♄ 205:46	♅ 217:20	♆ 250:50	♇ 10:22
☉ 172:59	54	125	82	6	103	305	328	316	283	163
☽ 33:34	275	345	302	227	324	166	189	177	143	24
☿ 161:19	43	113	70	354	91	293	317	304	271	151
♀ 168:15	50	120	77	1	98	300	324	311	278	158
♂ 203:19	85	155	112	36	133	335	359	346	313	193
♃ 225:45	107	177	134	59	156	358	21	9	336	216
♄ 99:46	341	51	8	293	30	232	255	243	210	90
♅ 68:35	310	20	337	262	359	201	224	212	178	59
♆ 94:20	336	46	3	287	24	226	250	237	204	84
♇ 184:53	66	137	93	18	115	317	340	328	295	175

empty fifth houses, suggesting that the two had parallel orientations toward life and that both were primarily focusing their energies within the same areas of experience.

The loose sextile aspect between Sand's fourth house sun and Chopin's sixth house sun signifies a basically relaxed and productive person-to-person contact carrying overtones of Sand's maternal and protective attitude (Cancer sun in the fourth) toward the fragile composer. Both have Venus in the sixth house, within a one degree conjunction; their association held much potential for sharing inner experiences and a mutual inclination toward self-criticism, introversion, and answers to life sought from within. These common characteristics were given opportunity to grow and were brought into the most intimate realms of interpersonal relatedness through a conjunction of the eighth house Jupiters that in turn form harmonious, responsive sextiles to the two Venuses.

A most significant contact exists between Sand's sun and Chopin's Saturn, involving the interpenetration of two phases. Sand's zodiacal sun is situated at 9°44′ Cancer (and in her fourth house, doubly emphasizing it in terms of personal integration and maternal instinct) while Chopin's house-oriented Saturn is located at 9:46 of the fourth house. That is, in terms of a 360-degree cycle of unfoldment, Sand's sun and Chopin's Saturn occupy the same place (the 100th phase of 360) against the background of two different frames of reference. Sand's sun occupies the 100th phase of a cycle of unfoldment that deals with energy differentiation (the zodiac); Chopin's Saturn is situated in the 100th phase of the cycle of unfolding experiences (the houses). This connection symbolizes that Sand's central solar purpose was motivated by a mode of energy that was parallel to the type of experience that defined and structured Chopin's sense of identity, and that there was an open channel for the exchange of these functions between the two. The Sabian symbol for Phase 100 (10° Cancer) sheds light on the meaning that such a close and unusual contact may have held for Sand and Chopin: "*A large diamond in the first stages of the cutting process*"; Rudhyar's keynote: "The arduous training for perfection in order to fully manifest an ideal."

This symbolic image suggests that through the sun-Saturn contact Sand and Chopin were able to participate, to some extent at least, in the early phases of a great work requiring both superior artistic craftsmanship and a vision of how things should be if an ideal were to be realized. The nature of the task that involved Sand's essential life purpose and Chopin's sense of form and definition, which no doubt permeated their entire relationship, was probably made most apparent through their substantial pioneering contributions to the arts. They did much to further the evolution of human consciousness by providing individuals with more relevant and sensitive models of expression. George Sand lived the life of a modern "liberated" woman a century and a half ago; Chopin's compositions paved the way for the musical innovations of our own era.

THE HOUSE TRANSPOSITION CHARTS

When Chopin's planets are placed within Sand's house structure, his Venus, sun, Pluto, and Mars fall into the first house—signifying that Sand experienced him in a very direct and immediate yet (because of the diversity of the planetary functions involved) complex manner. These four planets in Sand's first house also symbolize their ability to recognize and understand one another as individuals. In addition, Chopin's Venus is within a degree and a half of Sand's ascendant, symbolizing her potentiality to experience and bring out the artistic side of his nature, as well as to come in touch with his anima, his inner woman.

Chopin's natal Jupiter-moon opposition along with his lunar nodes are situated in Sand's second–eighth house axis, suggesting that the two had something to learn from each other concerning the use of resources and the exchange of human energies. The passionate and romantic nature of their liaison is symbolized by Chopin's moon falling into Sand's eighth house, and Sand's moon transposed into Chopin's eighth house.

George Sand's philosophical outlook and world view were no doubt deeply stimulated by Chopin with three of his natal planets, of diverse natures, situated in her ninth house. Here we find Uranus the transformer, universalizing Neptune, and conventionalizing Saturn. This arrangement would seem to suggest that while Sand's ex-

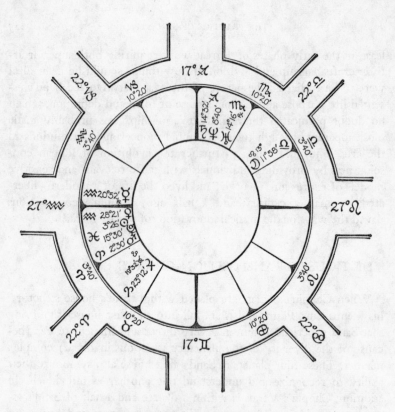

Sand's Houses—Chopin's Planets

pansive, synthesizing mind experienced the composer as exciting, not only because he was unusual and mysterious (Uranus retrograde in the fifteenth degree of Scorpio) but also because of his religious and sensitive (Neptune in Sagittarius) yet conservative and therefore challenging (Saturn) qualities.

When Sand's planets are placed within Chopin's house structure, only the fourth, fifth, and seventh houses are left vacant. Sand's Saturn is situated in Chopin's first house, suggesting that he experienced her both as a limiting element and as a giver of form and definition in terms of his personal life. Uranus and Jupiter fall into his second house, with the moon opposite them in the eighth, sig-

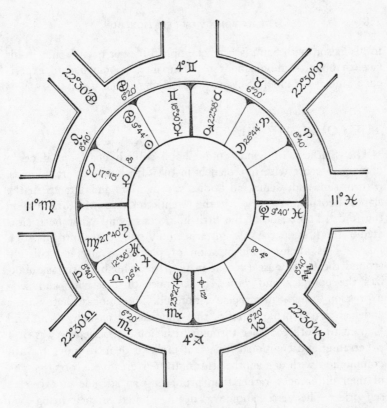

Chopin's Houses—Sand's Planets

nifying that the relationship with Sand may have altered or trans-
formed (Uranus) Chopin's attitude toward material living, yet it also
increased (Jupiter) the scope of his experience in this realm. Sand's
tight Neptune-Mars opposition is located in Chopin's third and
ninth houses, suggesting that her openness to life and love stimulated
him on a mental level (Neptune in his third) as well as his being
impressed, and possibly feeling threatened by, her high-minded philosophy and keen sense of understanding (Mars in his ninth). The
professional success and productivity their union brought them
could be denoted by Sand's Mercury in Chopin's tenth and her sun
in his eleventh houses. Finally, the involvement of Chopin's anima

in his liaison with Sand is further implied by her natal Venus in his twelfth house—symbolizing the potentiality Chopin had to experience Sand as a symbol of his own underlying anima.

THE COMPOSITE CHART

The synthesis of Sand's and Chopin's birth charts produces a composite chart with five planets in the fifth house: Mars, Uranus, Saturn, sun, and Venus, all bodies except Mars and Uranus in the sign of Scorpio. Mercury is in the twentieth degree of Libra, just on the fourth house side of the fifth house cusp, and Neptune is situated in the first degree of Sagittarius, only one degree into the sixth house. This intense concentration of planets in and immediately around the fifth house (vacant in both their birth charts) symbolizes the complex and varied experiences of creativity and self-expression brought into their relationship. The emphasis here on the zodiacal sign Scorpio signifies that the energy enabling Sand and Chopin to work together through fifth house experiences was of a penetrating and emotional type that inclined them to move toward communion with one another through their creative efforts, in spite of their differences, rather than promoting an attitude of excessive self-pride. Their association was deeply rooted in their being two creative individuals (fifth house) energized by deeply internal and emotional (Scorpio) sources.

The seventh house composite Jupiter in Capricorn indicates an expansive as well as enduring quality. Composite Pluto in Pisces very near the composite M.C. suggests that the liaison possessed extraordinary powers of regeneration and held within it a potential for evolving new forms of cultural ideals and values. The nourishing and adaptive qualities of their relationship are represented by the composite moon in the first house, Cancer.

The angles of the Sand-Chopin composite chart are particularly interesting. The local ascendant (arrived at by calculating the composite M.C. and referring to a table of houses for the corresponding ascendant for the latitude of Paris) is ten degrees Cancer—the exact position of Sand's natal sun as well as Chopin's house-oriented Saturn discussed a few paragraphs above.

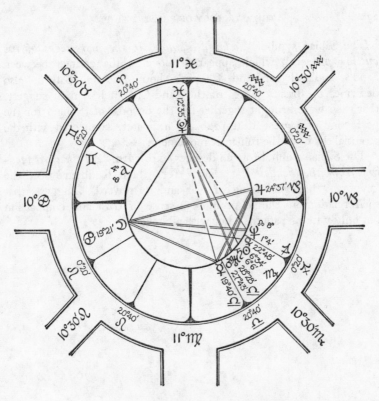

Sand-Chopin Composite Chart

	☉ 216°54'	☽ 109°21'	☿ 199°40'	♀ 232°48'	♂ 207°43'	♃ 294°37'	♄ 216°6'	♅ 208°28'	♆ 241°4'	♇ 342°35'
☉ 132:18		253	344	17	9	282	1	9	336	234
☽ 14:7	242		270	237	262	175	254	261	229	127
☿ 119:33	348	255		327	352	266	344	352	319	218
♀ 144:31	13	230	336		26	299	17	25	352	251
♂ 125:36	7	249	354	19		274	352	360	327	226
♃ 201:58	291	173	278	303	284		79	87	54	313
♄ 131:56	1	243	348	13	354	71		8	336	234
♅ 126:10	7	248	354	19	360	76	6		328	226
♆ 150:45	342	224	329	354	335	52	342	336		259
♇ 271:34	221	103	208	233	215	291	221	215	240	

The Sabian symbol "*A large diamond in the first stages of the cutting process,*" which appeared above in the contact between Sand's zodiacal sun and Chopin's house-oriented Saturn, also describes the basic "what" of the Sand-Chopin liaison. It suggests that they were brought together for the purpose of training for the perfection of a great ideal, probably intimately connected with the essential theme of the romantic movement.

The Sabian symbol for ten degrees Capricorn, "*An albatross feeding from the hands of a sailor,*" for which Rudhyar gives the keynote, "the overcoming of fear and its rewards," suggests that their relationship should promote a sense of trust and compassion not only with one another, but with all beings.

HELENA P. BLAVATSKY &
HENRY S. OLCOTT

H. P. BLAVATSKY: A NATAL PERSPECTIVE

Helena Petrovna Von Hahn was born August 12, 1831, at Eka-
terinoslav, Russia, at approximately 2:00 A.M. She has been described by her relatives as an exceptional person even in early childhood: "lively, highly gifted, full of humor and the most remarkable
daring . . . [with a] craving for independence and freedom of action," as well as having shown evidence of psychic powers and a
deep interest in the metaphysical world from the start. Her mother,
a feminist and novelist, died when Helena was only eleven years old.
After her mother's death Helena went to live in the home of her
well-to-do grandparents, where her dramatic and forceful personality was the distress of a succession of governesses. Just before her
seventeenth birthday, Helena was married to an elderly (or at least
much older) Russian politician, Nikifor V. Blavatsky. After three
months of living with him in what seems to have been a most intol-
erable situation and after a few unsuccessful attempts to escape,
Helena managed to leave and to convince her family that recon-
ciliation was out of the question.

Supported financially primarily by her father, Blavatsky spent the next approximately twenty-five years traveling extensively. As she did not keep a journal, and in later years was somewhat reluctant to recall the details of her early life, her biographers have pieced together a history that is sometimes inconsistent, and there are numerous contradictions in the various sources. She apparently went directly to Egypt upon leaving Russia, and also visited Africa, Turkey, and Greece, then lived in various places in Europe, traveled to Canada, Mexico, Central and South America, and to some of the Pacific Islands. She spent some time in New York and Chicago in 1854 and traveled by covered wagon with a group of emigrants to San Francisco in that year.

Countess Wachmeister, with whom Blavatsky worked closely during her later years, reports in her biography of Blavatsky that on her twentieth birthday, in London, Blavatsky for the first time physically met and spoke with her spiritual teacher, Morya Gulab, whom she immediately recognized as the guardian appearing in many of her childhood visions. Morya proposed that she help to organize what was to become the Theosophical Society—a vehicle for the expression of "Divine Wisdom"—a mission requiring some years of preparation in Tibet. There is evidence that her subsequent travels were primarily for the purpose of investigating the knowledge and traditions of ancient peoples all over the globe. After one or two unsuccessful attempts, she finally penetrated into Tibet, probably in 1856, and spent a number of years there on that and on subsequent visits, as well as in India, Nepal, and surrounding areas, with her teacher Morya and his colleague Koot Hoomi (usually referred to as the "Master M." and the "Master K.H.," or the "Mahatmas," in theosophical literature). According to H.P.B., as she preferred to be called after her occult apprenticeship was completed, these two Masters were members of the trans-Himalayan branch of an occult brotherhood composed of individual adepts or initiates of occult knowledge. These individuals have evolved beyond the known states of ordinary human consciousness; according to the Encyclopaedia Britannica, "in such adepts as Morya the spiritual nature is supposed to have been so developed that the [physical] body has become the ductile instrument of the intelligence, and they have thus gained a control over natural forces . . ." The brotherhood of adepts is in possession of ancient occult wisdom, and it is their responsibility to oversee human evolution on earth and do whatever they can to assist it—within certain limitations—in accordance with individual and collective karmic conditions. The tidal wave of materialism, technology, and religious dogmatism that was engulfing the entire planet in the nineteenth century was of particular concern to Morya and Koot Hoomi, and after many decades of searching for one capable of serving as their messenger to the Western world, they chose H. P. Blavatsky.

It is unfortunate that the exact time of Blavatsky's birth is not known. We are told by members of her family, however, that calamity surrounded her first moments. She was born several weeks prematurely and her relatives doubted that the puny infant would live more than a few hours. In order to provide her with the benefits of Christianity, a baptism was arranged within hours of her birth. The ceremony climaxed in a disaster: Helena's young aunt, standing in as proxy godmother, fell asleep as the Russian orthodox priest was reciting his incantation, dropping her ceremonial candle. Before anyone, including the priest, knew what was happening, the priest's robes were up in flames, seriously burning their occupant.

In the midst of all the excitement, Blavatsky's exact birth time was never accurately recorded. According to the general accounts left by those attending the birth, however, it seems certain that the sign of Cancer was on the eastern horizon, the birth taking place a few hours after midnight. Various astrologers have rectified her birth charts convincingly to several Cancer ascendants: one gives twelve degrees on the ascendant, another fifteen, another nineteen, and yet another twenty-eight degrees Cancer. The two that have gained the most recognition among both astrologers and students of Blavatsky are those with twelve and nineteen degrees Cancer rising.

I have chosen to use here the chart with nineteen degrees Cancer on the ascendant. Although there is not a great deal of difference among the proposed Cancer charts, the ambiguity (resulting in the possibility of an error of more than one or two degrees on the angles) does mean that the house-oriented positions of her natal planets, as well as the house-contact charts set up between herself and others, should be studied as general guides that very well may be several degrees off in terms of the angles.

Blavatsky's birth chart displays a distinct seesaw pattern: Her natal planets are arranged into two definite groups. One of the two planetary groups is situated in the personalizing lower hemisphere. This concentration is defined by a waxing/applying septile between the sun and moon. Its midpoint (fourteen Virgo) is close to Blavatsky's I.C., with the sun, Mars, Saturn, and Mercury east of the I.C. and Venus and the moon to the west. This massing of personal planets in the subjective lower hemisphere is brought into contrast by the congregation of the trans-Saturnian planets, as well as Jupiter, all retrograde and situated around the western, relationship-oriented side of the objectifying, collectivizing upper hemisphere. This group is bounded by the planets Pluto and Neptune. The center of gravity for this group (two Pisces) is close to an opposition aspect with the lower planetary group's center of gravity at fourteen Virgo.

The chart's planetary gestalt suggests a deep interplay between inner, personal, subject-oriented consciousness and consciousness in its relationship-oriented social mode. For H.P.B. one of life's greatest tasks was to combine these two modes of consciousness in a harmonious way that allowed for their mutual fulfillment. Symbolically speaking, she was challenged to integrate day and night. Although the angles of Blavatsky's chart are speculative, the zodiacal gravity center of the two planetary groups that compose the seesaw pattern does not vary significantly with regard to the time difference for any of the suggested Cancer ascendants.

The sun-moon midpoint of fourteen Virgo occupies a zodiacal space close to Blavatsky's natal Mercury, in the third house. This point symbolizes the basic nature of Blavatsky's subjective and personal energies, symbolizing how they could be most effectively brought into focus and constructively released. Mercury's proximity to this midpoint indicates that these personal energies flowed naturally through the Mercurial functions: writing, conversing, and the like. The Sabian symbol for fourteen Virgo gives added significance: "*An aristocratic family tree*"; Rudhyar's keynote being, "a deep reliance upon the ancestral roots of individual character." This statement refers not only to one's physical ancestry but also to the type of character that an individual has been developing during a series of incarnations and the support such characteristics can lend

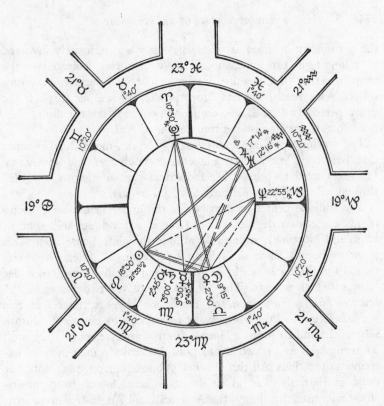

H. P. Blavatsky's Birth Chart

	☉ 138°30′	☽ 189°15′	☿ 159°30′	♀ 182°30′	♂ 152°45′	♃ 317°14′	♄ 153°0′	♅ 312°16′	♆ 292°55′	♇ 10°30′
☉ 41:30		51	21	44	346	182	346	187	206	128
☽ 102:36	62		30	7	37	233	37	237	257	179
☿ 71:1	30	32		337	7	203	7	208	227	149
♀ 97:22	56	6	334		30	226	30	231	250	172
♂ 61:31	342	42	10	36		196	360	201	220	143
♃ 219:48	182	243	212	238	202		165	5	25	307
♄ 61:52	340	41	10	36	360	158		201	221	143
♅ 212:42	189	250	219	245	209	7	210		20	302
♆ 185:31	216	278	246	272	237	35	237	28		283
♇ 283:34	118	180	148	174	138	297	139	290	262	

the personality in times of crisis. Blavatsky was intimately involved in a long-term project spanning many centuries dedicated to the transformation of humanity, involving not only herself but many others. As a result, she had "root power" to see her through the many personal turmoils and confrontations that she encountered in her efforts to accomplish her transcendental goal.

The waxing/applying septile linking the sun-moon dyad signifies that Blavatsky felt a very immediate (applying) and instinctual (waxing) need to pursue her individual path of destiny (septile) through all of her personal activities (sun-moon).

The zodiacal center of gravity for the upper hemispheric group of planets is two degrees Pisces (this is the indirect midpoint of Pluto and Neptune), which falls around the ninth house cusp. This point represents Blavatsky's basic orientation to others, her relationship to the outer world in general, and the dissemination of her transcendental message. The Sabian symbol for two Pisces is: "*A squirrel hiding from hunters.*" Rudhyar's keynote states that this symbol refers to "the individual's need both to ensure his future subsistence and to protect himself from aggressive social elements." The emphasis is on self-protection. Blavatsky's mission was extremely precarious. All through her public life, from 1874 until her death in 1891, she was under almost constant attack from materialistic scientists, the clergy, the American and Anglo-Indian governments, and sometimes from her friends and co-workers. She was a lone agent for an occult brotherhood, sent out into a culture hostile to the knowledge it was her function to disseminate. She was accused of being a Russian spy, a transvestite, the most devious and masterful fraud of the nineteenth century—the sole creator of everything connected with the Mahatmas.[2] In *The Mahatmas and Their Letters*, a treatise on Koot Hoomi and other adepts and their communications with the Anglo-English journalist A. P. Sinnett, Geoffrey Barborka writes:

People have, of course, questioned the existence of the Mahatmas. They argue: if the Mahatmas exist why do we not see them? Why should they refrain from coming into the world and showing their powers? Yet history shows what has happened to the remarkable personages who have appeared from time to time . . . Look what happened to Apollonius of Tyana!—He was imprisoned, so was Cagliostro. So would Saint-Germain have been, if had he not vanished from the scene. See what befell H. P. Blavatsky! Even now, after almost a hundred years, she is slandered; while calumnies are circulated by the news media in our day and age. [p. vii]

It was H. P. Blavatsky's purpose to gather around her the "seed people" of her time and to give out a teaching that had been up to that time most esoteric. At the same time she had to defend herself and the theosophical movement, for which she was the focus on the physical plane, against the attacks of those who felt threatened by her message or by her method of presenting it. Her natal Mars and Saturn opposing the upper planetary group's gravity center represent an inner strength, courage, and security that enabled her to hold steadfast in the face of severe antagonism. The Sabian symbol for this conjunction, three degrees Virgo, refers directly to the psychic reinforcement she received through her contact with Morya and Koot Hoomi. It reads: "*Two guardian angels*," with a keynote of "invisible help and protection in times of crisis."

H.P.B.'s chart contains a septile formation, composing three points of a seven-pointed star, connecting sun, moon, and Neptune. This configuration links the two bodies that define the lower planetary congregation with one of the two bodies that structure the upper group of planets. The sun-moon septile, discussed a few paragraphs above, is blended here with Neptune, symbolic of psychic phenomenon as well as transcendental experiences, situated near Blavatsky's natal descendant. Essentially, this sun-moon-Neptune pattern refers to Blavatsky's strong psychic abilities and her alliance with the occult brotherhood.

Blavatsky was a most gifted and prolific writer; hers is no doubt the finest attempt at explaining the inexplicable in modern language. The situation of Mars, Saturn, Mercury, and the part of fortune in the area of the third house, Virgo, signifies her great potential for writing along subjects that required great detail, while retaining a style of enthusiasm. Mercury is also the focus of a "yod" formation: two quincunxes from Mercury to Uranus and Pluto and a sextile between the latter planets. Here the scribe function (Mercury) is being made the focus of a relationship that combines with both harmony and tension the Uranian transformative function and the Plutonian function of essentialization and reformation of values.

HENRY S. OLCOTT: A NATAL PERSPECTIVE

The man who became H. P. Blavatsky's partner in the foundation of the Theosophical Society, Henry Steel Olcott, was born on August 2, 1832, at approximately 11:15 A.M. in East Orange, New Jersey.

From an early age, Olcott showed himself to be an achiever. He was internationally recognized as an authority on agriculture while still in his early twenties, having developed many new farming techniques and written two widely received books on agriculture. A few years later he became a successful newspaper reporter. With the outbreak of the Civil War, Olcott turned his investigative talents to running down dishonest businessmen who were making illegal fortunes in their dealings with the Army. For the great courage and impeccable morality he maintained throughout, he was given the rank of Colonel by the Union Army. Later he was selected with a few others to investigate the assassination of Abraham Lincoln. After his governmental duties were fulfilled he began practicing law and pursuing his favorite amusement since youth—spiritualist investigation—in his spare time.

In 1874 Henry Olcott met H. P. Blavatsky at the homestead of William and Horatio Eddy in Vermont. The Eddy brothers had been attracting a good deal of attention by their ability to materialize phenomena, and Olcott was there on a second assignment to investigate and report his findings for the *New York Graphic*. His reports, which established the validity of the phenomena to the best that his elaborate and thorough testing procedure could discover, were causing a world-wide stir of interest in spiritualism (copies of the paper were selling out immediately, some being scalped for a dollar a copy). These reports attracted Blavatsky to the scene, and her presence, evidently, caused even more extreme phenomenal occurrences. Olcott, whom Blavatsky described at the time as being a "rabid Spiritualist," was intrigued with the mysterious, powerful woman and the two soon became close friends.

Blavatsky was not herself a spiritualist, but rather an occultist. The support she gave to the spiritualists during the first few years of her public life, including many newspaper articles and letters written jointly by her and Olcott, was meant to encourage the very few who were beginning to accept outlooks other than the purely materialistic, although the unwillingness of most spiritualists to consider a philosophical investigation of the nature of the universe to explain occult phenomena eventually caused a rift between Blavatsky and the spiritualist movement. By that time, however, Olcott had aligned himself with Blavatsky and was ready to leave his family and his country in order to dedicate himself to the dissemination of the theosophical philosophy. Soon after this critical decision Olcott, as the president-founder of the Theosophical Society, moved with Blavatsky from New York City to India in 1879, where he toured, lectured, and managed the affairs of the Society until his death in 1907.

Olcott coupled his theosophical activities with work directed toward the regeneration of Asiatic religion and culture. He established schools and colleges in India and Ceylon where Buddhist and Hindu children would not be indoctrinated into nineteenth-century Christianity and Anglo life styles. He promoted a revival of Sanskrit and founded a large library of ancient and contemporary manuscripts dealing with oriental philosophy and religion.

The over-all perspective of Henry Olcott's birth chart reveals a seesaw pattern very similar to Blavatsky's—except with planets oriented so that they fit into the empty segments of Blavatsky's chart. This suggests that Olcott's more activated areas of experience are complementary to H.P.B.'s. The lower western group of planets in Olcott's chart spans 105 degrees from Neptune near the I.C. to Mars in the seventh house, Taurus. The upper eastern group is contained within a bi-novile that connects the tenth house sun in Leo to the Scorpio moon just below the ascendant. The two ends of Blavatsky's seesaw were clearly confined within separate horizontal hemispheres; Olcott has one planet of each group just into the other hemisphere. Of the group centered in the lower western portion of

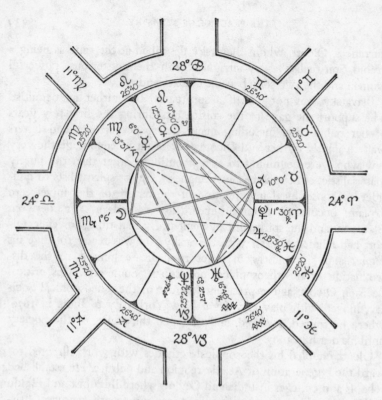

Henry S. Olcott's Birth Chart

	☉ 13°30′	☽ 211°6′	☿ 156°0′	♀ 132°30′	♂ 40°0′	♃ 358°30′	♄ 163°37	♅ 316°48′	♆ 295°22′	♇ 11°30′
☉ 283:5		81	26	2	91	132	327	174	196	119
☽ 6:48	84		56	79	172	213	48	255	276	200
☿ 309:46	27	58		24	116	158	353	200	221	.145
♀ 285:11	3	82	25		93	134	329	176	198	121
♂ 195:19	88	172	115	90		42	237	84	105	29
♃ 153:19	130	214	157	132	42		195	42	64	347
♄ 317:45	326	50	353	328	238	196		207	229	153
♅ 109:39	174	258	201	176	86	44	209		22	306
♆ 87:30	196	280	223	198	108	66	231	23		284
♇ 166:55	117	200	143	119	29	347	151	303	281	

the chart, only Mars penetrates into the upper half; of the congregation centered in the upper eastern part of the birth chart, only the moon is situated in the lower hemisphere. The seesaw configuration in this position denotes a strong sense of contrast between personal and objective modes of experience, along with the ability to understand and unify both within one's self.

Five of Olcott's natal planets are situated in fixed zodiacal signs, signifying a strong, determined character and a capacity for accomplishing goals through long-range plans. The placement of six planets in angular houses denotes powerful drives, initiative, and impulsiveness—it was Olcott who actually came up with the practical idea of forming a "theosophical society."

A powerful, confrontative T-cross links the harmonious conjunction of Olcott's sun-Venus in the tenth house, Leo, with an inner revolutionizing Uranus, retrograde, in the fourth house, Aquarius, and the focal, mobilizing Mars in the seventh house, Taurus. I see this configuration as a symbol of Olcott's potential for sensitive administrative abilities as well as his serving as an understanding father-image (sun-Venus in the tenth, Leo) for a large organization that had its roots in a revolutionary, transformative ideal, an ideal with the potential to totally change one's concept of self and one's relation to the universe (Uranus in the fourth house, Aquarius). The stress and tension that was created in order to fulfill such a function could be most effectively and constructively released by Olcott through the channel of his Mars function. Mars, situated as it is in the seventh house, Taurus, implies a very direct, down-to-earth quality to Olcott's manner of fulfilling the sun-Uranus opposition. He never professed to be a teacher but saw himself more as an executive. In their relationship, H.P.B. was the spiritual, metaphysical teacher and Olcott, the man who could stimulate others and create a focus for the communication of Blavatsky's message.

THE CHART OF THE THEOSOPHICAL SOCIETY

Soon after Blavatsky and Olcott met at the Eddy homestead, they began corresponding with large numbers of persons and receiving numerous visitors every evening, attracted by their many letters and articles to the press "on behalf of truth in Modern Spiritualism . . . to unveil what is, and to expose what is not." On September 7, 1875, an Egyptologist delivered a lecture to a group of people at H.P.B.'s apartment in New York. During the discussion that followed his presentation, Olcott passed a note to H.P.B. by way of William Quan Judge, a young lawyer who, along with Olcott, had been studying occult philosophy intensely under the guidance of H.P.B., suggesting that an organization be formed "for this kind of study." The first meeting in the public hall secured for the purpose, at which Olcott delivered his inaugural address, occurred at 8 P.M., November 17, 1875. The Society was formed to serve the following objects: (1) The formation of a nucleus of a universal brotherhood of humanity without distinction of race, creed, sex, caste, or color; (2) The study of ancient and modern religions, philosophies, and sciences, and the demonstration of the importance of such study; and (3) The investigation of the unexplained laws of nature and the psychical powers latent in man.

There are several possible times for which a chart of the Theosophical Society could be erected; its official birth as an independent, collective entity, however, has been traditionally considered to be the November 17 inaugural meeting. It is one of the most remarkable charts of the past century.

The map has a most distinct fourfold pattern—with all ten planets divided into four distinct groups. Every planet, with the exception of Venus at the tenth degree of Sagittarius, is located in a fixed zodiacal sign (and all four fixed signs are represented)—a most unusual and significant configuration. In addition, eight of the ten planets are placed in succedent houses and are very close to the zodiacal midpoints of the quadrants—areas of release for the dynamic energy built up in the quadrants.

The fourfold pattern, the fixed and succedent preponderances,

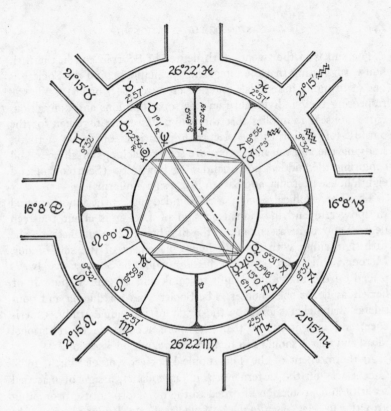

Theosophical Society's Birth Chart

and the great abundance of squares and oppositions all point to a most definite set of purposes (and cross purposes) and ideals. The over-all pattern of the chart implies that the Theosophical Society has a definite mission to fulfill and has a great deal of vital energy available for doing so, and that it will survive, at least in terms of form and organizational structure, the almost continual strife and conflicts that have been perpetrated within it over the past hundred years. Every "major" aspect in the Theosophical Society's chart, with the exception of a loose waning/separating trine between the sun and moon, is either a conjunction, a square, or an opposition. There are, in additon, a few quintile and septile aspects.

The sun is in the twenty-fifth degree of Scorpio and in the fifth house, suggesting that the integrating principle behind the Society is one of bringing individuals together as a group (Scorpio) while still respecting their individuality and personal opinions and convictions (fifth house). It implies that the group has come together for the purpose of exploring the deeper implications of group activity, studying the ancient and heretofore secret teachings of all ages, and exploring the hidden potentialities of humanity (Scorpio-sun and eighth house Mercury and Saturn in the sign Aquarius).

The Theosophical Society was founded just as the moon entered the powerful and individualistic sign of Leo—it is about fourteen degrees above the ascendant, in the first house. The emphasis on the fifth sign, along with the fifth house placement of the sun, Venus, Mercury, and Jupiter, reflects the high value the Society has always placed on the individual's right to think and to express himself or herself as he or she chooses. The Society has no dogma and considers "that belief should be the result of individual study, experience, and insight rather than the mere acceptance of traditional ideas, and that it should rest on knowledge, not on assertion."

At the moment of the Theosophical Society's official birth, 16°8′ Cancer was on the eastern horizon (ascendant), a sign of maternal security and protection afforded to the new born entity, promoting growth. In *An Astrological Mandala*, Dane Rudhyar gives the Sabian symbol for this degree as, "*The unfoldment of multilevel potentialities issuing from an original germ.*" And, indeed, the Theosophical Society was the "original germ" from which every subsequent esoteric or occult organization has evolved during the past century, many of them being direct split-offs organized by one-time members and leaders of the Theosophical Society.

The chart of the Theosophical Society is relevant both as a horary chart in Blavatsky's and Olcott's development (its founding being the external culmination of a line of activity on their part) and as a map of their "offspring": a distinct, yet collective entity of their making. There are several interesting connections between the chart of the organization and those of its two most prominent founders. Blavatsky's natal sun is very near the T.S.'s Uranus and linked by a tight opposition to its Mars and Saturn, which are, in turn, conjunct her natal Jupiter. Olcott's Uranus at seventeen Aquarius and his sun and Venus situated in mid-Leo are also linked with this configuration. Olcott, Blavatsky, and the Theosophical Society seem to have been tapping the same extremely dynamic source of zodiacal energy that is at its apex at the middle of the fixed signs and the focal, succedent houses. These four fixed points have been regarded as channels of the descent of cosmic energy as well. Concerning the significance of these points, Rudhyar writes in *The Astrology of Personality*:

It is evident that the points of maximum release of energy are to be found midway between equinoxes and solstices [and the angles]. These points are thus on the following degrees of the circle: 45-135-225-315; or in terms of the usual zodiacal nomenclature: Taurus 15; Leo 15; Scorpio 15; Aquarius 15. These points are not unknown to some occultists. They correspond to what has been called: the Four Gates of Avataric Descent. As an "Avatar" in ancient terminology is in fact a *release of cosmic power*, the meaning of the phrase is quite evident. These Four Gates are symbolized by the four symbolic creatures: the Bull—the Lion—the Eagle—the Angel. Each of them depicts a particular type of dynamic release, a particular type or Ray of Power—and of power-releasing "initiation." [pp. 239-240]

The first major event in the history of the Theosophical Society after its creation in 1875 was the writing, under extraordinary circumstances (see Volume One of Olcott's *Old Diary Leaves* for more details), of *Isis Unveiled: A Master-Key to the Mysteries of Ancient and Modern Science and Religion* (in two volumes) by H. P. Blavatsky and its publication during the months of September and October of 1877. *Isis Unveiled* was an immediate success: The first printing of a thousand copies was completely exhausted within ten days of publication, and the books aroused much interest in theosophy and H.P.B., attracting many persons to the movement. These events were taking place just as the Theosophical Society's progressed sun and moon were approaching their third-quarter phase—the waning square that symbolizes release of a catalyst for the transformation of consciousness to a new level, transcending established structures and confines imposed in the past. The transformation may or may not have actually taken place around November 13, 1877 (the exact date of the progressed third-quarter moon) within the collectivity of persons known as the Theosophical Society, but it is clear that H. P. Blavatsky and the Theosophical Society were just beginning to effectually fulfill this function (as a catalyst for transforming consciousness) for Western culture.

H.P.B. and Olcott had planned to move the center of the theosophical operation to India for some time before they actually sailed to India via England on December 18, 1878 (with transiting Mars exactly conjunct the T.S.'s natal sun, and transiting Saturn opposite Olcott's Saturn). Having received instructions from Morya and Koot Hoomi, they left William Judge in charge of holding things together in New York. On December 17, 1882, after a few years in Bombay and touring Asia, they found a permanent base at Adyar, just outside of Madras in the south of India, where the international headquarters of the Theosophical Society has remained since.

In 1885 Blavatsky left India for Germany and later England where she undertook the writing of her *magnum opus, The Secret Doctrine*, in two volumes, *Cosmogenesis* and *Anthropogenesis*, broadly outlining a coherent picture of cosmic and human evolution. *The Secret Doctrine* was published during December 1888 when transiting Saturn was conjunct both her natal sun and the T.S.'s natal Uranus, and when the T.S.'s progressed sun was exactly conjunct its natal Venus. The work is now almost universally recognized as the foundation of occult and ancient knowledge in the modern world.

After long and serious illnesses H.P.B. left the physical plane of existence on May 8, 1891, in London, England (while transiting sun was square her natal sun and Venus conjunct her Pluto; with the T.S.'s progressed moon exactly semi-square its natal M.C.). There was a conjunction of Neptune and Pluto at this time, a conjunction that occurs once every five hundred years. H.P.B., it has been said, can be regarded as a seed of the previous five-hundred-year cycle, which began at the end of the fourteenth century with the close of the Medieval Order in Europe and the beginnings of the Humanist Movement and the Renaissance.

After H.P.B.'s passing, the theosophical movement went through a confused state (from which it has not yet totally emerged), and eventually many differences of opinion surfaced that led to splits of all sorts over the years—some of which were initiated by W. Q. Judge, Alice Bailey, Rudolph Steiner, Jeddu Krishnamurti, and Max Heindel. The Theosophical Society, however, has survived and prospered in spite of constant conflicts and difficulties, and if we are to believe what H. P. Blavatsky said almost a hundred years ago, the next few years may be an important time for both the Theosophical Society and the world at large.

THE ZODIACAL CONTACT CHART

The state of humanity in 1875 was characterized by scientific rationalism and materialism (the emphasis on material needs and concurrent de-emphasis of spiritual values), the supremacy of Western nations on the international scene, and religious intolerance. It was a time when there was almost no doubt that Western civilization and technology were the spearhead of human achievement and would elevate the entire world from its misery, poverty, and ignorance. The white male person recognized himself as the highest creature on the evolutionary scale. He thus believed it was up to him to "enlighten" the savages of uncivilized lands by introducing Western life styles and religion to all corners of the globe. As recompense for his efforts in this direction, he claimed the right to exploit material resources and native labor as a means of fulfilling his ever-increasing thirst for power, materials goods, and absolute supremacy in the physical realm of existence.

Perhaps at the pinnacle of "success" in the material world, Victorian man was on the verge of spiritual bankruptcy. The notion of brotherhood, particularly with people of other races and creeds and, of course, women, was largely thought to be an impractical, naïve dream—and a most unprofitable course. The thought that there might be any superphysical order or purpose behind the materialistic evolution advanced by Charles Darwin was considered both "unscientific" and ridiculous by the intellectual community—and, in turn, religious leaders held that any theory of evolution, physical or spiritual, was heresy. The idea of there being realms of existence beyond normal human sensory perception (as Blavatsky demonstrated) was considered to be either superstitious or the work of the devil, depending upon whether one's persuasion was scientific or religious.

Only a few persons of the late nineteenth century were able to anticipate the repercussions and deeper implications of the strictly materialistic view of life. Indeed, many people today are just beginning to awaken to a world beyond materialism—and there remain those who promote industry and business at the expense of the ecological balance of the planet and the welfare of humanity. Two of the few who felt it imperative to awaken Western civilization to a purpose beyond the material were H. P. Blavatsky and H. S. Olcott.

Most of both Blavatsky's and Olcott's planets in their zodiacal contact chart are distributed around the same areas of zodiacal space. Blavatsky has six planets between mid-Leo and mid-Libra, while Olcott has five planets within the span of mid-Leo to early Scorpio; Blavatsky's remaining planets are situated between late Capricorn and mid-Aries, while the remaining five planets of Olcott's chart are located between late Capricorn and mid-Taurus. This arrangement indicates that the two were tapping similar energy sources and were able to identify with one another's way of using these respective energies. The fact that Blavatsky's and Olcott's suns are only a few degrees apart in mid-Leo suggests that they held in common a central source of vital energy that molded their inner sense of strength, courage, pride, and strong drives toward self-expression. Their Leo suns also point to abilities for leadership as well as love of theatrical, personal displays.

There is a sextile aspect between Blavatsky's moon in the tenth degree of Libra and Olcott's sun in the eleventh degree of Leo signifying an extremely productive and harmonious association, in spite of occasional differences of opinion that are bound to arise between two such individualistic Leo types. The basic purpose upon which their entire relationship was founded was that of fulfilling a

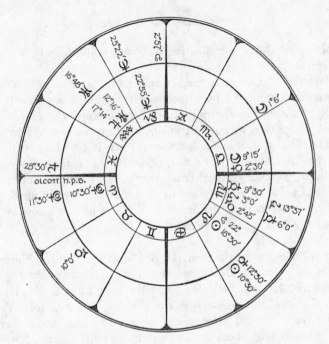

Blavatsky-Olcott Zodiacal Contact Chart

	☉ 138°30'	☽ 189°15'	☿ 159°30'	♀ 182°15'	♂ 152°45'	♃ 317°14'	♄ 155°0'	♅ 312°16'	♆ 292°55'	♇ 10°30'
☉ 130°30'	352	302	331	308	338	174	338	179	198	120
☽ 211°6'	73	22	52	29	59	254	59	259	279	201
☿ 156°0'	18	327	357	334	4	199	3	204	224	146
♀ 132°30'	354	304	333	310	340	176	340	181	200	122
♂ 40°0'	262	211	241	218	248	83	247	88	108	30
♃ 358°30'	220	170	199	176	206	42	206	47	66	348
♄ 163°37'	26	335	5	342	11	207	11	212	231	154
♅ 316°48'	179	128	158	135	165	360	164	5	24	307
♆ 295°22'	157	107	136	113	143	339	143	344	3	285
♇ 11°30'	233	183	212	189	219	55	219	60	79	1

planetary need—the introduction of occult knowledge to the Western world.

Blavatsky's function as teacher and author needed to be complemented and promoted by someone who, while being sensitive and totally dedicated to the purpose of Morya and Koot Hoomi, possessed exceptional executive and organizational abilities. The sextile between Blavatsky's moon and Olcott's sun is a perfect symbol for this type of complementary association. In one of the phenomenally produced communications[3] from Morya and Koot Hoomi to A. P. Sinnett, at that time the editor of one of India's largest newspapers, Morya wrote, in 1882, that in their efforts to initiate a new cycle of occult research in the West they

> found in America the man [H. S. Olcott] to stand as leader—a man of great moral courage, unselfish, and having other good qualities. He was far from being the best, but (as Mr. Hume speaks in H.P.B.'s case)—he was the best one available. With him we associated a woman of most exceptional endowments. Combined with them she had strong personal defects, but just as she was, there was no second to her living fit for this work. We sent her to America, brought them together—and the trial began. From the first both she and he were given to clearly understand that the issue lay entirely with themselves. And both offered themselves for a trial for certain remuneration [of a spiritual type] in the far distant future. [*The Mahatma Letters to A. P. Sinnett*, p. 259]

Whereas Olcott was chiefly responsible for external matters, Blavatsky was more attuned with the inner, occult, and metaphysical implications of their association. It was Blavatsky who, in the early years of their relationship, gradually introduced Olcott to the purpose and significance of their working together.

In a letter to Olcott from Koot Hoomi the distinctions between the functions of Blavatsky and Olcott are stressed:

> H.P.B. has next to no concern with administrative details, and should be kept clear of them, so far as her strong nature can be controlled. But this *you must tell all: With occult matters she*

has everything to do . . . She is *our direct agent.* [*Letters from the Masters of Wisdom,* p. 53]

Blavatsky's sun is connected with Olcott's moon by a waxing/ separating quintile aspect, adding a creative quality to their association. Blavatsky's Uranus forms a close opposition to Olcott's sun and Venus, suggesting that their contact encouraged a transformation of his essential self-image and inner values.

One more point of interest in the zodiacal contact chart are the numerous septiles linking Blavatsky's and Olcott's planets. Septiles link Blavatsky's Mercury to Olcott's moon, her Venus to his sun, and her Pluto to his Neptune. Tri-septiles connect Blavatsky's Mars and Olcott's Jupiter, her Saturn and his Jupiter, and her Uranus to his Mercury. This proliferation of septiles is probably a symbol for the unusual, eccentric, and transcendental qualities that permeated many areas of their association and the global, planetary significance of their work together.

HOUSE CONTACT AND HOUSE TRANSPOSITION CHARTS

Because of the uncertainty of both Blavatsky's and Olcott's birth times, an interpretation of their house contact and house transposition charts is a highly speculative task. These charts are illustrated here, however, as a head start for those who would like to explore more deeply in spite of these possible limitations.

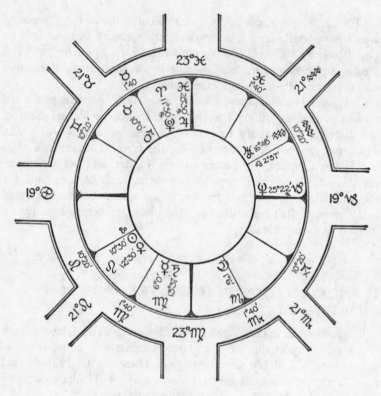

Blavatsky's Houses—Olcott's Planets

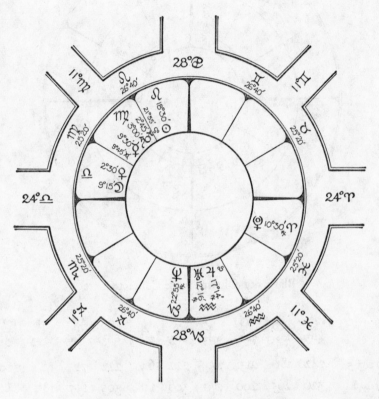

Olcott's Houses—Blavatksy's Planets

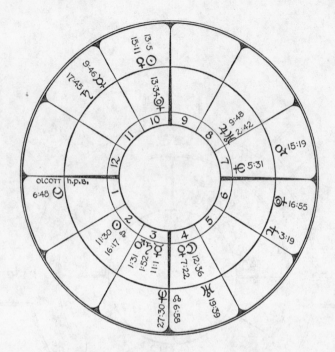

Blavatsky-Olcott House Contact Chart

	☉ 41:30	☽ 102:36	☿ 7:11	♀ 97:22	♂ 61:31	♃ 219:40	♄ 61:52	♅ 212:42	♆ 185:31	♇ 283:34
☉ 283:5	242	181	213	186	222	64	222	71	98	360
☽ 6:48	326	265	296	270	306	148	305	155	182	84
☿ 309:46	269	208	239	213	249	91	248	98	125	27
♀ 285:11	244	183	215	188	224	66	224	73	100	2
♂ 195:19	154	93	125	98	134	336	134	343	10	272
♃ 153:19	112	51	83	56	92	294	92	301	328	230
♄ 317:45	277	216	247	221	257	99	256	106	133	35
♅ 109:39	69	8	39	13	49	250	48	257	285	187
♆ 87:30	46	345	17	351	26	228	26	235	262	164
♇ 166:55	126	65	96	70	106	308	106	315	342	244

THE COMPOSITE CHART

Like the natal charts it is derived from, the Blavatsky-Olcott composite chart has a seesaw planetary pattern, with eight planets in the western hemisphere of relationship with others, and only the moon and Saturn in the eastern half. If the angles of the birth charts are reasonably accurate, the late degrees of Scorpio-Taurus are on the meridian with a composite ascendant in the seventh degree of Virgo. The local composite ascendant computed for Madras, India, the focal center of their physical energies from 1880 onward, is twenty-five Leo. These angles denote the strong, steadfast nature of their relationship. The composite sun and Uranus are conjunct, with an orb of only two minutes of an arc in the fifteenth degree of Aquarius, in the sixth house of personal reorientation and service. They are trine to the second house moon, providing them with a vision of how to present their revolutionary message in a practical and comprehensive fashion. That there were deep karmic implications of their work in serving the needs of a new age (sun-Uranus in the sixth house, Aquarius) is suggested by the tri-septile linking the sun-Uranus pair to the first house, Saturn.

The fifteenth degree of Aquarius is a particularly intense part of the zodiac, a point of release for cosmic energy flowing toward the manifestation of new forms of individual and collective interrelationships. The composite sun in this degree symbolizes the centering and integrating function of the Blavatsky-Olcott relationship, vitalized by such energies. The close conjunction the sun makes with Uranus, significator for the sign Aquarius, greatly intensifies this situation. The Sabian symbol for the fifteenth degree Aquarius is of interest here: "*Two lovebirds sitting on a fence and singing happily*"; Rudhyar's keynote: "The blessing bestowed upon personal achievements by the spiritually fulfilled consciousness of the Soul."

Another striking feature of the Blavatsky-Olcott composite chart is the conjunction of Venus, Mercury, and Jupiter in the seventh house of social contacts in the eighth degree of Pisces. This concentration contributes varied and complex functions (those of inner evaluation, communication, and preservation to the relationship

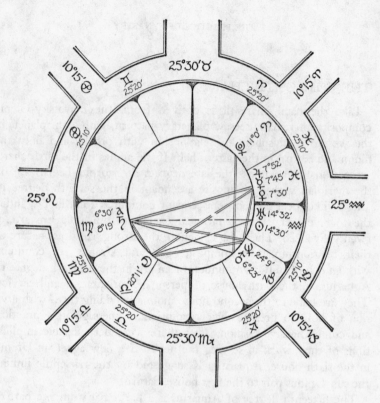

Blavatsky-Olcott Composite Chart

	☉ 314°30'	☽ 200°11'	☿ 337°45'	♀ 337°30'	♂ 276°23'	♃ 337°52'	♄ 158°19'	♅ 314°32'	♆ 294°9'	♇ 11°0'
☉ 170:12		246	24	23	39	337	157	360	21	304
☽ 55:13	246		223	223	284	223	42	246	267	190
☿ 193:24	24	222		1	62	360	180	24	44	327
♀ 193:9	23	223	1		62	360	180	24	44	327
♂ 131:30	322	284	62	62		299	119	322	343	266
♃ 193:31	337	222	360	360	298		180	24	44	327
♄ 13:57	157	42	180	180	18	180		204	225	148
♅ 170:45	360	245	23	23	321	23	204		21	304
♆ 149:33	21	266	44	44	342	44	225	22		284
♇ 226:9	305	190	328	327	266	328	148	305	284	

existing between the Blavatsky-Olcott pair. The close opposition between these three planets and composite Saturn in the first house suggests that they were able to bring into clear focus their combined energies (Saturn in the first house) for the purpose of stimulating the spiritual growth of others (Venus, Mercury, and Jupiter in the seventh house, Pisces).

The Sabian symbol for the eighth degree of Pisces beautifully describes the primary function of the Blavatsky-Olcott union in terms of their relationship with others: *"A girl blowing a bugle."* Rudhyar's keynote interprets this as "a call to participation in the service of the race, as an evolutionary crisis approaches."

NOTES

1. See *The Interpretation of Nature and the Psyche* by C. G. Jung.

2. Much of the literature concerning the life and work of H. P. Blavatsky is inaccurate, some of it actually hostile. Biographers differ greatly in their characterizations of her, while many of her followers attempt to conventionalize and whitewash her. The most reasonable accounts include *When Daylight Comes* by Howard Murphet (Theosophical Publishing House, 1975); *Personal Memoirs of H. P. Blavatsky* compiled by Mary K. Neff (original edition, 1937; current edition: Theosophical Publishing House, 1967); H. S. Olcott's *Old Diary Leaves* Vols. I and II (Madras, India: Theosophical Publishing House, 1895 and 1900; 1941 and 1954); and *H. P. Blavatsky and the Theosophical Movement* by Charles J. Ryan (original edition, 1932; current edition, San Diego: Point Loma Publications, 1975).

3. A thorough exposition of the significance and extraordinary production of the series of communications to A. P. Sinnett and others known as "The Mahatma Letters" can be found in *The Mahatmas and Their Letters*, Geoffrey A. Barborka (Madras, India: Theosophical Publishing House, 1973). Complete transcriptions of the 145 letters to A. P. Sinnett are to be found in *The Mahatma Letters to A. P. Sinnett*, compiled by A. T. Barker (Madras, India: Theosophical Publishing House, 1923, 1962).

BIBLIOGRAPHY

I. ASTROLOGY

Jones, Marc Edmund. "Arabian Astrology," a study course (Stanwood, Wash.: Sabian Publishing Society, 1932–33).

——. *Essentials of Astrological Analysis* (New York: Sabian Publishing Society, 1960).

——. *The Guide to Horoscope Interpretation* (Stanwood, Wash.: Sabian Publishing Society, 1941, 1969).

——. "Pythagorean Astrology," a study course (Stanwood, Wash.: Sabian Publishing Society, 1929).

——. *The Sabian Symbols in Astrology* (Stanwood, Wash.: Sabian Publishing Society, 1953, 1969).

——. "Symbolical Astrology," a study course (Stanwood, Wash.: Sabian Publishing Society, 1931).

Rudhyar, Dane. *The Astrological Houses: The Spectrum of Individual Experience* (Garden City: Doubleday & Company, Inc., 1972).

——. *An Astrological Mandala: The Cycle of Transformations and its 360 Symbolical Phases* (New York: Random House, 1973).

——. *An Astrological Study of Psychological Complexes and Emotional Problems* (The Netherlands: Servire, 1969).

——. *Astrological Timing* (New York: Harper & Row, 1972).

——. *The Astrology of Personality* (New York: Lucis Press, 1936; Garden City: Doubleday & Company, Inc., 1970).

——. *The Lunation Cycle* (The Netherlands: Servire, 1967; Berkeley: Shambhala, 1971).

——. *My Stand on Astrology* (Palo Alto, Calif.: The Seed Center, 1972).

——. *Person-Centered Astrology* (Lakemont, Ga.: CSA Press, 1973).

——. *The Practice of Astrology* (The Netherlands: Servire, 1968; Baltimore: Penguin, 1970).

——. *The Pulse of Life* (New York: David Mackay, 1943; The Netherlands: Servire, 1963; Berkeley: Shambhala, 1970).

——. *Triptych* (The Netherlands: Servire, 1968).

——. various articles in *Horoscope* and *American Astrology*, 1934 to date.

II. PSYCHOLOGY

Arthur, Gavin. *The Circle of Sex* (New Hyde Park, N.Y.: University Books, 1966).

Assagioli, Roberto. *Psychosynthesis* (New York: The Viking Press, 1965).

Frankl, Viktor E. *Man's Search for Meaning: An Introduction to Logotherapy* (Boston: Beacon Press, 1959; New York: Pocket Books, 1963).

Jacobi, Jolande. *The Psychology of C. G. Jung* (New York: Harper & Row, 1971).

Jaffe, Aniela. *From the Life and Work of C. G. Jung* (New York: Harper & Row, 1971).

Jung, C. G. *Analytical Psychology* (New York: Random House, 1970).

——, ed. *Man and His Symbols* (Garden City: Doubleday & Company, Inc., 1964).

——. *Memories, Dreams, Reflections* (New York: Random House, 1961).

——. "Synchronicity: An Acausal Principle." In *The Interpretation of Nature and the Psyche*, Bollingen Series (New York: Pantheon Books, 1955).

Maslow, A. H. *The Farther Reaches of Human Nature* (New York: The Viking Press, 1971).

——. *Religions, Values, and Peak-Experiences* (New York: The Viking Press, 1970).

Rogers, Carl R. *On Becoming a Person* (Boston: Houghton Mifflin, 1961).

de Ropp, Robert S. *Sex Energy* (New York: Dell Publishing Company, 1971).

Singer, June. *The Boundaries of the Soul* (Garden City: Doubleday & Company, Inc., 1973).

Whitmont, Edward C. *The Symbolic Quest* (New York: G. P. Putnam, 1969; Harper & Row, 1973).

III. OCCULT PHILOSOPHY

Bailey, Alice A. *Initiation, Human and Solar* (New York: Lucis Publishing Company, 1944).

Barborka, Geoffrey A. *The Mahatmas and Their Letters* (Madras, India: Theosophical Publishing House, 1973).

Barker, A. T. compiler, *The Mahatma Letters to A. P. Sinnett* (Madras, India: Theosophical Publishing House, 1923, 1962).

Bercholz, Hazel Silber, ed. *Maitreya 5* (Berkeley, Calif.: Shambhala Publications, 1974).

Blavatsky, H. P. *Isis Unveiled* (Pasadena, Calif.: Theosophical University Press, 1877, 1960).

——. *The Key to Theosophy* (Pasadena, Calif.: Theosophical University Press, 1889, 1972).

——. *The Secret Doctrine*, 2 vols. (Pasadena, Calif.: Theosophical University Press, 1888, 1963).

Bragdon, Claude. *A Primer of Higher Space* (The Fourth Dimension) (Tucson: Omen Press, 1972).

Hall, Manly P. *The Secret Teachings of All Ages* (Los Angeles: The Philosophical Research Society, 1928, 1971).

Hanson, Virginia, ed. *H. P. Blavatsky and the Secret Doctrine* (Wheaton, Ill.: Theosophical Publishing House, 1971).

Hartmann, Franz. *Paracelsus* (New York: John W. Lovell, 1891, 1963).

Kaltenmark, Max. *Lao Tzu and Taoism* (Palo Alto, Calif.: Stanford University Press, 1969).

Krishna, Gopi. *The Awakening of Kundalini* (New York: E. P. Dutton, 1975).

Leadbeater, C. W. *Man, Visible and Invisible* (Madras, India: Theosophical Publishing House, 1902, 1964).

———. *The Chakras* (Madras, India: Theosophical Publishing House, 1927, 1968).

Michell, John. *City of Revelation* (London: Garnstone Press, 1972).

———. *View Over Atlantis* (London: Sago Press, 1969).

Plummer, L. Gordon. *The Mathematics of the Cosmic Mind* (Wheaton, Ill.: Theosophical Publishing House, 1970).

Rudhyar, Dane. *Directives for New Life* (Railroad Flat, Calif.: Seed Publications, 1971).

———. *Occult Preparations for a New Age* (Wheaton, Ill.: Theosophical Publishing House, 1975).

———. *The Planetarization of Consciousness* (New York: Harper & Row, 1972).

The Secret of the Golden Flower, translated and explained by Richard Wilhelm (New York: Harcourt, Brace & World, 1931, 1962).

Smuts, Jan Christiaan. *Holism and Evolution* (New York: Macmillan, 1926; New York: The Viking Press, 1961).

Steiner, Rudolf. *An Outline of Occult Science* (Spring Valley, N.Y.: Anthroposophic Press, 1972).

———. *Cosmic Memory* (Blauvelt, N.Y.: Steiner Books, 1959, 1971).

Taylor, Thomas. *The Theoretic Arithmetic of the Pythagoreans* (New York: Samuel Weiser, 1816, 1972).

Waley, Arthur. *The Way and Its Power* (New York: Grove Press, 1958).

Welch, Holmes. *Taoism: The Parting of the Way* (Boston: Beacon Press, 1957, 1965).

IV. BIOGRAPHICAL

Eek, Sven. *Damodar and the Pioneers of the Theosophical Movement* (Madras, India: Theosophical Publishing House, 1965).

Encyclopaedia Britannica (Chicago: Encyclopaedia Britannica, Inc., 1973).

Endersby, Victor A. *The Hall of Magic Mirrors: A Portrait of Madame Blavatsky* (New York: Carlton Press, 1969).

Jung, C. G. *Memories, Dreams, Reflections* (New York: Vintage Books, 1961, 1963).

Murphet, Howard. *When Daylight Comes: A Biography of Helena Petrovna Blavatsky* (Wheaton, Ill.: Theosophical Publishing House, 1975).

——. *Hammer on the Mountain: The Life of Henry Steel Olcott (1832–1907)* (Wheaton, Ill.: Theosophical Publishing House, 1972).

Neff, Mary K. compiler. *Personal Memoirs of H. P. Blavatsky* (Wheaton, Ill.: Theosophical Publishing House, 1937, 1967).

Olcott, H. S. *Old Diary Leaves*, Vol. I–III (Madras, India: Theosophical Publishing House, 1895, 1972).

Ryan, Charles. *H. P. Blavatsky and the Theosophical Movement* (San Diego: Point Loma Publications, 1975).

Wehr, Gerhard. *Portrait of Jung* (New York: Herder and Herder, 1971).

Winwar, Frances. *George Sand and Her Times* (New York: Lancar Books, 1945, 1972).